14+

BREAK THROUGH to CLIL

T0344210

for

Physics

David Sang
Timothy Chadwick

CAMBRIDGE
UNIVERSITY PRESS

Contents

Introduction   4

1 **Making measurements**   **6**
   Exercise 1.1 Quantities and how they are measured   6
   Exercise 1.2 Quantities and units   8
   Exercise 1.3 Measuring density   9

2 **Describing motion**   **14**
   Exercise 2.1 Movement – word definitions   14
   Exercise 2.2 Interpreting the shape of a graph   15
   Exercise 2.3 Making comparisons   16
   Exercise 2.4 Changing speed   17
   Exercise 2.5 Acceleration – interpreting questions   18
   Exercise 2.6 A journey by coach   20

3 **The effects of forces**   **21**
   Exercise 3.1 Mass and weight   21
   Exercise 3.2 Moments and stability   24
   Exercise 3.3 Stretching springs   26
   Exercise 3.4 Pressure   29

4 **Energy and work**   **31**
   Exercise 4.1 Recognising forms of energy   31
   Exercise 4.2 Energy transfers   33
   Exercise 4.3 Where we get our energy from   35
   Exercise 4.4 Energy resources   37

5 **Thermal physics**   **39**
   Exercise 5.1 Kinetic theory vocabulary   39
   Exercise 5.2 Explaining changes   40
   Exercise 5.3 Instructions for calibrating a thermometer   41
   Exercise 5.4 Thermal expansion – drawing conclusions   43
   Exercise 5.5 Heat transfer – interpreting diagrams   45

6 **Sound and waves**   **48**
   Exercise 6.1 Making sounds   48
   Exercise 6.2 Describing sounds   49
   Exercise 6.3 Oscilloscope traces   51
   Exercise 6.4 Range of hearing experiment   53
   Exercise 6.5 Representing waves – interpreting graphs   54

7   Light and other electromagnetic radiation   **57**
Exercise 7.1 Words, symbols and definitions   57
Exercise 7.2 Refraction of light   59
Exercise 7.3 How a lens works   61
Exercise 7.4 The discovery of infra-red radiation   62
Exercise 7.5 The electromagnetic spectrum   64

8   Magnetism and static electricity   **67**
Exercise 8.1 Words and meanings   67
Exercise 8.2 Magnetic fields   69
Exercise 8.3 Static electricity – describing, observing and explaining 70

9   Electric circuits   **73**
Exercise 9.1 Electric current: words and meanings   73
Exercise 9.2 Interpreting graphs   75
Exercise 9.3 Describing an experiment   77
Exercise 9.4 Electrical components   78
Exercise 9.5 Electrical safety   80

10   Electromagnetism   **82**
Exercise 10.1 Oersted's discovery   82
Exercise 10.2 Making motors more powerful   83
Exercise 10.3 Describing an experiment   85
Exercise 10.4 Using transformers   87

11   Atomic physics   **89**
Exercise 11.1 Atomic structure   89
Exercise 11.2 Elements and isotopes   91
Exercise 11.3 Background radiation   92
Exercise 11.4 Alpha, beta, gamma   94
Exercise 11.5 Handling radioactive substances   96

Answer key   98
Language file   114

Introduction

Note to students

Welcome to this workbook, which will help you with your study of physics using English. To progress well in your studies in physics, it will help if you can also use the English language well in a way that is appropriate to science. If you can read English well, you can understand what is written in your physics textbook easily. If you can write and speak English well, you can share your knowledge about physics with others easily.

This workbook will help you understand some important topics in physics. It will also help you develop your skills in English. The exercises will give you practice in both things at the same time.

The exercises will help your English skills in different ways. They will:

- help you understand the meaning of important words
- help you to use certain types of words correctly, like nouns and adjectives
- help you to construct sentences correctly
- help you to construct whole passages of text
- give you practice in reading text and extracting information from it.

Each unit in this book covers a different area of physics, but almost exclusively covers the Core IGCSE topics. You do not need to complete all the units in the order in which they appear in the book. Instead, as you are being taught a certain area of physics in the classroom, you should complete the exercises in the unit that covers that area. Your teacher may ask you to work on the exercises at home or in class.

Throughout the text you will see language boxes like this one. These boxes give you some background information about the English language skills that you are learning about. If you see the icon ( ), this means you can read more about that area of English language in the *Language File* at the back of this book.

> A *rule* is the same as a *ruler*. It is a special term used for a ruler that is one metre long.

You will also find an *Answer Key* for the exercises at the back of this book. You can use this to check whether your answers are correct. Sometimes there are many different possible answers to a question. The *Answer Key* will make it clear that the suggested answer is just an example, and your own answer might look different. In these cases, look carefully at the structure of your answer, to see if it is the same as the answer in the *Answer Key*. There are notes in the *Answer Key* that will help you to see if your answer is a correct one. If you are still not sure, then ask your teacher to help you.

We hope you enjoy using this book, and that you progress well in your studies of Physics and English.

The Breakthrough to CLIL team

Note to teachers

This book is designed to help EAL/ESL/E2L students understand the content of their physics course and build English language skills within the context of their physics studies, though you may also use it to support students who have English as their first language. It is intended for use within the context of a physics course, rather than an English course, but almost exclusively covers the Core IGCSE topics. If your school has an embedded CLIL or bilingual programme, you may find this book suitable to support most or all of your students in their studies. However, this book can also be used as part of your differentiation for a smaller number of students who would benefit from it, whether in the classroom or as homework.

The areas of physics covered in this book are the basic topics that most students aged around 14 to 16 would encounter. However, most students would also be expected to be familiar with some other topics, as well as covering the topics included in this book in more detail. The intention of this book is to help students master the basics, and develop language skills and confidence that will help them in other parts of their course. This book should be used to support a wider learning programme that also includes a textbook of an appropriate level.

The areas of English language covered in this book have been selected for their relevance to understanding and discussing the subject of physics. Where aspects of language are discussed explicitly, this is intended to help students understand the purpose of certain exercises, as well as explain why these aspects of language are relevant to physics. It is expected that the students will be able to link these explanations to the content of their English language (or E2L) course. We hope that you as a physics teacher will feel confident enough in the areas of language discussed to support your students, with the help of the explanations provided in the text and the Language File. If not, we advise you to discuss the content of this book with a colleague in your English department.

Each unit of this book covers a certain area of physics. Within each unit, the level of demand in terms of both physics and English gradually increases. This will allow students to build understanding and language skills as they progress through each unit. The first exercise in each unit does require some familiarity with key vocabulary and concepts, so we recommend that you begin to set the exercises in this book after having taught a lesson or two on the relevant topic. The units have been designed to be used independently from one another, so you can set them in any order to match your existing teaching programme.

We hope that you will enjoy using this book with your students.

The Breakthrough to CLIL team

1 Making measurements

This unit covers:

- ☐ quantities and measurement
- ☐ quantities and units
- ☐ density.

Exercise 1.1 Quantities and how they are measured

> This exercise checks that you understand some of the important words we use when we take measurements in physics.

1 John wanted to measure the length of a block of wood. He used a ruler. In his notebook, he wrote:

length of block = 22.4 cm

a Complete the third column in the table using information from the text above.

Term	Definition	Example from text above
quantity	something that can be measured	
measuring instrument	a device used to measure a quantity	
value	the result of measuring a quantity	

b The value of a quantity has both a number and a unit. What is the unit of length in the text above?

....

2 We use different measuring instruments to measure different quantities.

a Complete the first two columns of the following table using the words from the list.

temperature   ruler   measuring cylinder   clock   volume
length   time   thermometer

Measuring instrument	Quantity measured	Unit

b In the third column of the table, write the unit name for each quantity.

c Turn each row of the table into a sentence. Here is an example:

A ruler is used to measure length in centimetres.

....

....

....

....

....

....

3 In her notebook, Siti described how she measured the volume of a pebble. She didn't use appropriate scientific words. She wrote:

We filled a water cylinder half-way up. We wrote down the amount it said. To find out how big the pebble was, we put it under the water and wrote down the new amount. We worked out the difference between the two amounts.

Rewrite Siti's description. Use words from this list to replace some of Siti's words.

immersed   **calculated**   **volume**   **measuring cylinder**
half-filled   **recorded**   **determine**

Use words from this list to help give structure to your description.

First,   **Next,**   **After that,**   **Then,**   **Finally,**

....

....

....

....

....

....

....

Exercise 1.2 Quantities and units

In this exercise, you will practise using ideas about quantities and units.

In physics, it is important to record measurements correctly. Remember that each value has two parts:

- a number
- a unit.

1 Read the text below. Draw a circle around each value mentioned.

It was a hot day – over 30 °C. We had to walk 5 km to get home. It took 2 h because we kept stopping for water. I drank more than 1.5 dm³. I had to carry a box with 10 kg of tins of food inside it.

2 Complete the table to show the quantities that are mentioned in the text and their values. In the third column, write the full name of each unit. The first row has been done for you.

Quantity	Value	Unit
temperature	30	degree Celsius (°C)

3 Scientists usually use standard units called SI units. Metres, kilograms and seconds are examples of SI units.

Each unit has a symbol, for example 'g' *stands for* grams – by this we mean 'g' represents or means 'grams'.

The size of a unit can be changed by adding a prefix in front of the symbol. For example, 'k' stands for 'kilo-', which means one thousand. A kilogram (kg) is one thousand grams.

Take care! The letter 'm' can stand for a unit. It can also stand for a prefix.

a In the unit cm, what does the prefix 'c' stand for?

....

b What unit is represented by 'm'?

....

c What does 'm' stand for when it is a prefix, for example in 'ms'?

....

d What does the symbol 'mm' stand for?

....

e Give the names and symbols for two units of mass.

....

f Give the names and symbols for two units of length which are smaller than a metre.

....

g What does the symbol 'ms' stand for?

....

h Which is bigger, 1 ms or 1 μs?

....

i What quantity can be measured in m^3 and cm^3?

....

Exercise 1.3 Measuring density

The idea of density allows us to compare different materials. In everyday life, we might say, 'Steel is heavier than plastic'. In science, we say, 'Steel is denser than plastic'. If we take one centimetre cubed of steel and the same volume of plastic, the steel will have a greater mass. Take care! We have to think about mass (g or kg), not weight.

1 The density of water is $1\,g/cm^3$. We say, 'one gram per centimetre cubed'. The word 'per' means 'for each'. This is shown by the solidus (/) in the unit.

a We can write: density of water = $1000\,kg/m^3$. Write this in words.

....

b We can write: the density of water is one kilogram per decimetre cubed. Write this unit in symbols.

....

If we think about the unit of density, this will help us to see how to calculate density.

c What quantity is measured in grams?

....

d What quantity is measured in centimetres cubed?

....

e Think about the unit of density, g/cm^3. This will help you to decide which of the following is the correct equation for calculating density. Draw a circle around it.

$$\text{density} = \text{mass} \times \text{volume} \qquad \text{density} = \frac{\text{volume}}{\text{mass}} \qquad \text{density} = \frac{\text{mass}}{\text{volume}}$$

If we know the densities of two or more materials, we can compare them using *adjectives*.

Adjectives are used to describe nouns, or 'things'. To compare two nouns, you need to use the **comparative** form of the adjective. For example, *longer* is the comparative form of *long*. It is followed by *than*.

This is a *long* book. It is *longer* than the Chemistry book.

We can also use the **superlative** form of the adjective when we mean something is the 'most'. *Longest* is the superlative form of *long*. In general, to make a superlative we use *–est* for small words like 'long', or *most* for longer words like 'expensive'.

If an adjective ends with 'y', we use *–ier* and *–iest* to make the comparative and superlative.

This book is the *longest* in the bookshop. Also, it is the *most expensive*.

2 In each example below, there are three sentences. Underline the adjective in the first sentence. Then fill the gaps in the second and third sentences using the comparative and superlative forms of the adjective. The first has been done for you.

Hydrogen is a <u>light</u> gas. It is *lighter* than helium. It is the *lightest* gas in the Periodic Table.

a John is lifting heavy weights. The red weight is .... than the blue one. The green one is the .... weight of all.

b Today we have experienced high winds. The wind today has been .... than yesterday. Tomorrow we will experience the .... winds this month.

c The pressure is low today. Tomorrow it is forecast to be .... The .... pressures are usually during the winter.

d Gold is a dense metal. It is .... than silver. Osmium is the .... metal in the Periodic Table.

3 This table shows the densities of some different metals. Use the information in the table to answer the questions that follow.

Material	Density (kg/m³)
aluminium	2700
copper	8900
lead	11 300
steel	7700
tin	7300

a Which is the densest metal?

....

b Is copper denser or less dense than steel?

....

c Density can be 'high' or 'low'. Which metal has the lowest density?

....

d Is the density of tin higher or lower than the density of steel?

....

e Which metal has a lower density than tin?

....

f Density of gold = 19 300 kg/m³; density of silver = 10 500 kg/m³; density of platinum = 21 400 kg/m³. Write different sentences comparing these metals.

....

....

....

....

....

....

4 Here are the instructions for measuring the density of a piece of steel.

- Fill a measuring cylinder halfway with water.
- Record the volume of the water.
- Find the mass of the cylinder.
- Immerse the steel in the water.

- Record the volume of the water again.
- Weigh the cylinder again.

Imagine that you have done this experiment. Rewrite the instructions as a paragraph describing what you did. The first sentence has been done for you.

First, we filled a measuring cylinder halfway with water. Next, ...

....

....

....

....

....

....

This is a good way to describe an experiment. However, an even better way is with the **passive voice** in the **simple past**. This is how a scientist would describe an experiment.

How do we make a sentence passive?

There are three simple steps. Here is an active sentence:

> We recorded the volume of water again.

To make this active sentence passive:

1 Find the object of the sentence. The object is the 'thing' that the verb is acting on: *the volume of water*. This becomes the subject of the new sentence.

2 Choose between *was* or *were*. You use *was* if the object is singular and *were* if it is plural. So in this case: *was*.

3 Next, use the **past participle** of the verb. When you see three forms of a verb given – such as *take/took/taken* – the past participle is the third form. The past participle of to record is: *recorded*.

This gives you the passive sentence:

> *The volume of water was recorded again.*

We use the passive voice in science because *what is happening* is more important than who is doing the action.

5 Now, rewrite the paragraph you wrote for question **4**. This time, use the passive voice in the simple past. The first sentence has been done for you.

First, a measuring cylinder was filled halfway with water. Next, ...

....

....

....

....

....

....

....

2 Describing motion

This unit covers:

- describing how things move
- distance–time graphs
- describing changing speed.

Exercise 2.1 Movement – word definitions

This exercise checks that you understand some of the important words we use to describe how objects move.

To write full definitions a bit like the ones in an English dictionary, we can connect a term to its definition using the words 'which' and 'that'. The part of the sentence following 'which' or 'that' is called a **defining relative clause**. In this case, 'which' and 'that' mean the same and either can be used. For example:

Copper is a material *which/that* has a density of 8900 kg/m³.

1 Here are nine words connected with how we describe movement. Separate the words using a solidus (/). The first one has been done for you.

speed/distancemotiondeceleratemetregradientcalculateequationaccelerate

2 The table below contains nine definitions. Use each word from **1** in the correct space in the table to make a full definition. Again, the first one has been done for you.

	Word	Definition
a	An equation is a formula	*that* shows how two or more quantities are related.
b	To .... is a verb	*which* means to work out a numerical value.
c	The .... is a noun	*that* tells us how steep a graph is.
d	A .... is a noun	*that* is a unit of distance.
e	.... is a noun	*which* tells us how far something has moved.
f	.... is a noun	*which* tells us how fast something is moving.

g	To .... is a verb	*that* means to slow down.
h	To .... is a verb	*which* means to go faster.
i	.... is a noun	*which* is another word for 'movement'.

Exercise 2.2 Interpreting the shape of a graph

A distance–time graph is a useful way of representing how an object moves. In this exercise, you will use words which describe a graph as well as words which describe motion.

This distance–time graph represents a car's journey along a road.

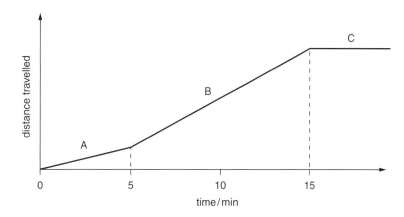

Look at these statements. The first statement is about the gradient (slope) of the graph. The second statement is about what the graph tells us about how the car moved.

> In section A, the gradient of the graph is not very steep.
>
> The distance between the car and its starting point is increasing slowly.
>
> Therefore, at first, the car is travelling slowly.

Now complete these descriptions of sections B and C in a similar way.

1 How does the graph change in section B?

In section B, the gradient of the graph ....

This shows that the car is travelling ....

2 How does the graph change in section C?

In section C, the gradient of the graph ....

This shows that the car is ....

Exercise 2.3 Making comparisons

When you talk about how objects move, you often need to compare the movements of different objects. In this exercise, you will practise using the correct language when making comparisons.

Three children ran in the local sports day.

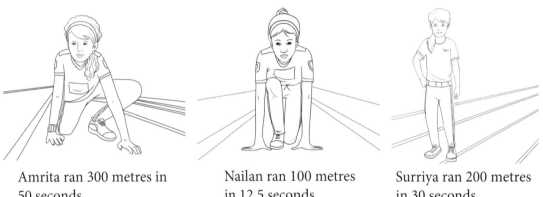

Amrita ran 300 metres in 50 seconds

Nailan ran 100 metres in 12.5 seconds

Surriya ran 200 metres in 30 seconds

1   Calculate the average speed for each child.

        Amrita   Nailan   Surriya

Remember: $\text{speed} = \dfrac{\text{distance travelled}}{\text{time taken}}$

2   Read each sentence below and decide whether it is correct. If a sentence is incorrect, cross out the word in bold and write a word on the line to make it correct. The first has been done for you.

Nailan ran ~~slower~~ than Amrita.
           faster

a   The distance run by Surriya was **longer** than the distance run by Amrita. ....

b   Nailan ran the **shortest** distance of all. ....

c   Nailan ran for a **longer** time than Surriya. ....

d   Amrita ran for the **shortest** time of all. ....

e   Surriya's average speed was **higher** than Nailan's. ....

f   Although Amrita ran for the **greatest** distance, her average speed was the **highest** of all. ....

Exercise 2.4 Changing speed

There are many ways of describing the motion of an object. In this exercise, you will read some descriptions of objects moving. You have to decide how their speed is changing.

1 In physics, it is important to know if an object's speed is changing.

In the table below, the first column describes how a car is moving. You have to decide whether the car is accelerating, decelerating or moving at constant speed. Tick the correct column. The first one has been done for you.

Description	Constant speed	Accelerating	Decelerating
moving at a steady speed	✔		
going faster			
slowing down			
travelling at 30 m/s			
speeding up			
coming to a halt			
increasing speed			
changing speed from 40 m/s to 20 m/s			
travelling 25 m each second			

2 A speed against time graph shows us when an object's speed is changing. The graph below shows how a car's speed changed during a short journey.

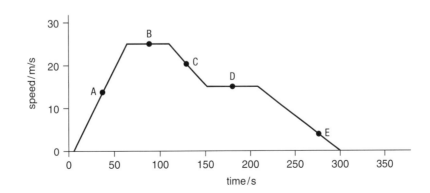

For each of the points marked on the graph, state what the graph tells you about the car's speed. Use words and phrases from the table in question **1**. Do not use the same word or phrase more than once.

A ....

B ....

C ....

D ....

E ....

Exercise 2.5 Acceleration – interpreting questions

Acceleration, speed and time are related to each other. In this exercise, you will need to interpret the questions to decide which of these quantities you have to calculate.

To answer the following questions, you will need the equation:

$$\text{acceleration} = \frac{\text{change in speed}}{\text{time taken}}$$

A *quantity* is something that can be measured or calculated (see exercises 1.1 and 1.2). So, this equation contains three quantities.

1 In an advertisement, a car is described like this:

'It can accelerate from 0 km/h to 80 km/h in 10 s.'

Calculate how much its speed increases in 10 s.

a Which quantity from the equation do you have to calculate? ....

Underline the words in the question that tell you that this is the quantity to be calculated.

b Calculate this quantity.

2 A cyclist is travelling at 4 m/s. She speeds up to 16 m/s in a time of 4.8 s. Calculate the rate at which her speed is increasing.

    a Which quantity from the equation do you have to calculate? ....

       Underline the words in the question that tell you that this is the quantity to be calculated.

    b Calculate this quantity.

3 A stone falls with an acceleration of 10 m/s^2. Calculate how much faster it is falling after 3.5 s.

    a Which quantity from the equation do you have to calculate? ....

       Underline the words in the question that tell you that this is the quantity to be calculated.

    b Calculate this quantity.

4 On the Moon, the gravitational field strength is weaker than on Earth. A stone falls from rest with an acceleration of 1.6 m/s^2. Calculate how long it will take to reach a speed of 10 m/s.

    a Which quantity from the equation do you have to calculate? ....

       Underline the words in the question that tell you that this is the quantity to be calculated.

    b Calculate this quantity.

Exercise 2.6 A journey by coach

In this exercise, you will interpret information describing a journey by coach, and present the information in a table and as a graph.

Read this description of a coach journey:

> The coach left the bus station at 13:00 p.m. It drove slowly at first, reaching the edge of town after 30 minutes. It had travelled 5 km. Next, it travelled along the motorway, covering 85 km in one hour. It left the motorway and travelled 15 km along a country road. At 14:50 p.m. it arrived in a village square where it waited for 10 minutes before setting off back to the town.

1 The coach journey was in four sections. Complete the table to show the times and distances for each section of the journey. The first row has been done for you.

Section	Clock time at end	Time taken / h	Distance travelled / km	Average speed / km/h
bus station to edge of town	13:30	0.5	5	5 / 0.5 = 10
motorway				
country road				
village square				

2 Now complete the last column of the table by calculating the coach's average speed for each section of the journey.

3 On the grid below, draw a speed–time graph for the journey. Label the four sections of the journey.

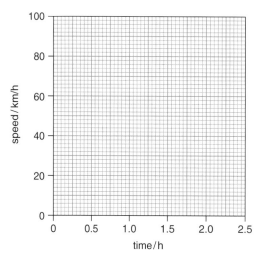

3 The effects of forces

This unit covers:

- mass and weight
- moments and stability
- stretching springs
- pressure.

Exercise 3.1 Mass and weight

This exercise checks that you understand the difference between mass and weight, two important quantities in physics.

1   The table below shows some statements about the quantities 'mass' and 'weight'. For each statement, decide whether it applies to mass, to weight, or to both. Show your answers by putting ticks in the boxes in the final two columns. The first example has been done for you.

Statement	Mass	Weight
… is a force.		✔
… is the pull of the Earth's gravity on an object.		
… has the symbol m.		
… is the amount of matter something is made of.		
… has a direction.		
… is measured in kilograms.		
… is measured in newtons.		
… can be represented by an arrow.		
… decreases when an object travels out into space.		

2 Most of the statements in question **1** are *descriptions* of mass or weight, but two are *definitions* of these quantities. A *definition* gives us a short but complete meaning of something. A *description* gives us extra information and details about something.

Write the two definitions here:

Mass is ....

....

....

Weight is ....

....

....

To **contrast** means to say how two things are different from each other. If we want to contrast two things, we can write two statements with a word in the middle to make the contrast. Those words we can use are '*but*', '*while*' and '*whereas*', and they all mean the same thing when used like this. For example:

Water is a liquid *but/while/whereas* ice is a solid.

Silver conducts electricity *but/while/whereas* plastic does not.

3 Complete these two contrasting sentences which tell us about important differences between mass and weight:

a If you go to the Moon, your mass stays the same …

....

b Mass is measured in kilograms …

....

4 When an object is dropped, its weight pulls it downwards. This makes it accelerate.

The diagram shows a ball falling. Its position is shown every 0.1 s.

a On the diagram, mark the position of the ball at the start.

b Now mark the distance it falls in 0.5 s.

c Explain how you can tell from the diagram that the ball is accelerating as it falls.

We know that the ball is accelerating because ....

....

....

....

....

....

Exercise 3.2 Moments and stability

> In this exercise, you will practise using ideas about the turning effect of a force, centre of mass and stability. These are important ideas which we use to explain why things happen.

In physics, we use words that are carefully defined. They are often related to words which we use in everyday speech.

1 In each sentence below, there is a word printed in bold. For each of these words, write an alternative word or phrase that means the same. You might need to use a dictionary.

a It was a **momentous** day when we reached the top of Mount Everest.

Alternative word or phrase: ....

b After the accident I woke up with a **massive** lump on my head.

Alternative word or phrase: ....

c The baby was very **unstable** because she had just learnt to walk.

Alternative word or phrase: ....

2 Each of the words in bold has a physics word hidden in it. Write these words on the line below.

....

3 Copy these physics words into the table below, in the space next to its definition.

Physics word	Definition
	the amount of matter in an object
	the turning effect of a force
	describes an object which will not easily fall over

4 We can use the ideas of *centre of mass* and *turning effect* to explain why some objects are more stable than others.

- The centre of mass of an object is the point at which we can consider its weight acting. An object with a low centre of mass and a wide base will be stable (less likely to fall over).

- A force can make an object turn (rotate). The bigger the force and the further it is from the pivot, the greater its turning effect.

We use the word *because* to introduce an explanation – *why* something happens. Complete the statements below so that the second half explains the first half.

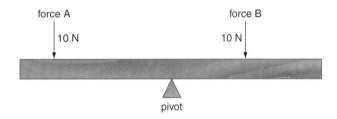

a Force A has a greater turning effect about the pivot than force B because …

....

....

b Object A is more stable than object B because …

....

....

Exercise 3.3 Stretching springs

Forces can change an object's shape. The object may be stretched or compressed. In this exercise, you will use the correct scientific terminology to describe these effects.

1 Read the following paragraph.

If you push or pull an object, its shape will change. For example, when you kick a football, it becomes squashed. If you stretch a rubber band, it gets longer. Pushing or pulling more, makes the shape change more.

Now complete the sentences below using words or phrases from the list to fill the gaps. This will give the same information using correct scientific terms.

compressed   become deformed   exert a force on   deformation

increasing the force   extends

a If you .... an object, it will

....

b For example, when you kick a football, it becomes ....

c If you stretch a rubber band, it ....

d .... will increase the ....

2 Using words from question **1**, give the scientific words which mean the same as the following verbs:

a to get longer = to ....

b to squash = to ....

c to change shape = to ....

d to become more = to ....

The diagrams show what happens when a weight is hung on the end of a spring. The spring gets longer.

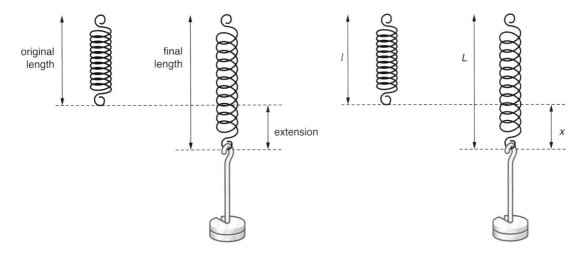

The diagram on the left shows what we mean by *extension* of the spring. The diagram on the right shows the same information in symbols.

3   Complete the table showing the symbol for each length.

Length	Symbol
original length	
final length	
extension	

4   It is important to understand what we mean by the extension of the spring. Read each statement below. Put a tick (✓) if the statement is correct; put a cross (✗) if it is incorrect.

   a   The extension is the increase in length of the spring. ....

   b   final length = original length + extension ....

   c   To calculate the extension, subtract the final length from the original length. ....

   d   The extension is calculated by subtracting the initial length from the final length. ....

   e   extension = final length – initial length ....

   f $x = L - l$ ....

   g   The increase in length of the spring is equal to the extension. ....

5 The picture shows the equipment used in an experiment to find out how a spring stretches when weights are attached to it.

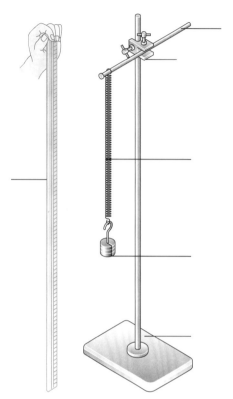

a Label the diagram using these words:

clamp stand	boss	metal rod
long spring	hanger with weights	
metre rule		

> A *rule* is the same as a *ruler*. It is a special term used for a ruler that is one metre long.

b Write instructions which will tell someone how to carry out this experiment. You should use some or all of the verbs from the list below. The first sentence has been done to help you.

hang	attach	measure	hold	clamp	add repeat

Clamp the metal rod in the boss.

....

....

....

....

....

....

Exercise 3.4 Pressure

This exercise helps you to understand some of the important words regarding the idea of pressure.

Read the following paragraph. It is a summary of ideas about pressure.

If you stand on an empty drink can, you will crush it. This is because a large force (your weight) is pressing on a small area, so the pressure is high. Fluids also exert pressure. For example, a swimming pool must be strongly built. If it is not, the pressure of the water will damage it. The pressure is greatest at the bottom of the deep end because there is more water pressing down from above. If you climb a mountain, the atmospheric pressure will get less. This is because there is less air above you, pressing downwards. If you look at a barometer on a mountain, you will observe that the height of the mercury column decreases.

1 Read the paragraph again. Underline any scientific words related to pressure that you find in the text.

In the paragraph, many of the facts are presented using **conditional sentences**. Conditional sentences often start with the word '*If*'. In this paragraph, the **first conditional** is used.

The first conditional is made of

'*If*' + present tense, + '*will*' + the infinitive (the basic form of the verb)

For example

If you *stand* on an empty drink can, you *will crush* it.

In science, we use the first conditional to describe facts we are certain of if an action happens.

2 The table below gives the meanings of several words or phrases related to pressure. Complete the table by adding the correct words in the first column. (They are all included in the paragraph above.)

	Word or phrase	Meaning
a		calculated as force/area
b		the force of gravity on an object
c		a liquid or a gas – any substance that will flow
d		the pressure of the air
e		an instrument used for measuring pressure

3 Alok lives in a house with a flat roof. The roof is not very strong. Alok's football has gone on the roof and Alok is rescuing it.

To avoid damaging the roof, Alok is crawling along a wooden plank to reach the ball.

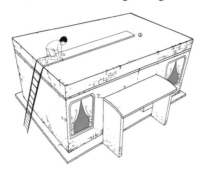

Explain how this will help to avoid damaging the roof. Use the following words in your explanation:

pressure   weight   force   area

You will find useful information to help you if you look back at previous exercises.

a   If Alok stands on the roof, ...

....

....

....

b   If Alok crawls on a plank, ...

....

....

....

4 Energy and work

This unit covers:

☐ forms of energy
☐ energy transfers
☐ energy resources.

Exercise 4.1 Recognising forms of energy

> The idea of energy is very important in science. You need to be able to name each form and say how you recognise it.

The name of each form of energy starts with an adjective. For example:

kinetic energy

The word 'kinetic' is an adjective which describes the noun 'energy'. Kinetic is a term which means 'related to movement'.

1 Here are ten words used to name forms of energy. First, you will have to separate the words in the string. Write the words in the spaces below. (The last one is a phrase of two words.) The first one has been done for you.

kinetic/thermalchemicalstrainlightsoundnuclearinternalelectricalgravitationalpotential

.... kinetic .... energy   .... energy

.... energy   .... energy

.... energy   .... energy

.... energy   .... energy

.... energy   .... energy

2 The table below contains descriptions of six forms of energy. Complete the table by writing the name of each form in the first column. The first one has been done for you.

	Form of energy	Description
	kinetic energy	is the energy of a moving object
a		is energy released in a chemical reaction
b		is energy stored in a hot object
c		is energy stored when an object is pushed upwards
d		is energy moving around an electric circuit
e		is energy released in a nuclear reaction

To recognise different forms of energy, we have to look for clues. For example:

- Uranium is used as fuel in some power stations.
- Its energy is released in a nuclear reaction.
- Therefore, we describe it as a store of nuclear energy.

> The word *therefore* shows that we have deduced the last statement from the first two. *Therefore* means 'That's why…'.

3 Here are seven similar statements about two other forms of energy. They are mixed up. Sort them out and write two paragraphs. In the first, explain how we know when an object has kinetic energy. In the second, explain how we know when an object has chemical energy. You will need to use the word 'therefore' in each paragraph.

It is a store of kinetic energy.

Its energy is released when it burns.

Many people use coal as a fuel.

It is moving.

A bus is travelling along a road.

It is a store of chemical energy.

Burning is a chemical reaction.

a Kinetic energy:

....

....

....

b Chemical energy:

....

....

....

....

4 Now write a third paragraph to explain how you know that a stretched rubber band is a store of strain energy.

....

....

....

....

Exercise 4.2 Energy transfers

Energy can move about from place to place. When energy moves, we say it is being *transferred*. There are several ways this can happen. This exercise helps you to use the correct terms to describe energy transfers.

1 Here are six words used when we are talking about energy transfers.

heat   work   light   sound   thermal   electrical

Use these words to complete the sentences below. First, you will need to separate the words of each sentence string. Here is an example to help you:

Energy/that/we/can/hear/with/our/ears

...is called sound... energy.

a Energythatwecanseewithoureyes

.... energy.

b Energythatisbeingtransferredinanelectriccircuit

.... energy.

c Energythatistransferredwhenaforcepushesanobject

....

d Energythatisspreadingoutfromahotobject (two words)

.... energy and .... energy.

2 You can use ideas about energy to describe what happens when we use a torch (also called a flashlight) to see in the dark.

a Use words from the list below to label the diagram of the torch.

switch   **battery**   **bulb**   **connecting wire**   **outer case**

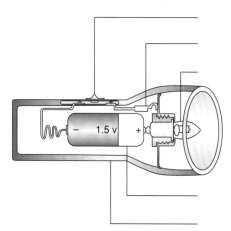

In science questions, you will be given **command words**. These are verbs that tell you what to do in the question.

'*State*' and '*describe*' are common examples of command words.

State means you should give a short answer with no explanation.

Describe means either:

- you should write what you can see in a graph, diagram or table (do not *explain* the data), or

- you should write down the steps that happen in a process.

b State how energy is stored in the torch when it is switched off.

....

....

c Describe the energy transfers that happen when the torch is switched on.

....

....

....

Exercise 4.3 Where we get our energy from

> People use energy for many different things – heating, lighting, operating machines, transport and so on. We use many different energy resources. In this exercise, you will interpret information provided in a pie chart.

The pie chart shows the different energy resources used by people around the world. Each sector of the chart shows the contribution of an energy resource.

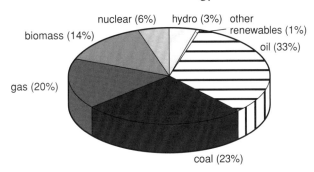

Biomass is the common name for organic materials that can be used as renewable energy sources such as wood, plant matter and crops.

In Exercise 1.3, we looked at comparing and contrasting things using comparative adjectives. We can also compare things using a comparative structure followed directly by the thing or noun. These comparative structures are:

less ... than   more ... than   the most   the least   as much ... as

For example:

Modern houses need *less heat than* old houses because they have better insulation.

I don't use *as much electricity as* you because I am very careful not to waste it.

1 Study the chart and decide if each of the following statements is correct or incorrect. If you think the statement is incorrect, cross out the words that are wrong and write the correction on the line below. Here is an example to help you:

We use ~~less~~ coal than biomass.

.... more ....

a The energy resource we use the most is oil.

....

b We use more gas than coal.

  ....

c We use twice as much hydro as nuclear.

  ....

2 In question **1**, you have seen some different phrases we use for comparing quantities or amounts. These include:

less … than   **more … than**   **as much … as**   **the most**   **the least**

Write sentences of your own using these phrases, together with information from the pie chart. Your sentences must all be correct!

a less … than

  ....

  ....

b more … than

  ....

  ....

c as much … as

  ....

  ....

d the most

  ....

  ....

e the least

  ....

  ....

Exercise 4.4 Energy resources

There are many different energy resources which we can use to generate electricity – fossil fuels, sunlight, the wind and so on. To choose the best one, we need to be able to *evaluate* them, and to *compare* one resource with another.

In the following exercise, you will be asked to 'evaluate', 'compare' and 'explain' a range of energy resources.

'Evaluate' means to consider the advantages and disadvantages of something.

'Compare' means to say what is the same or different about two or more things.

'Explain' means to say how and why something happens.

1 Tim and Huda have been discussing the best way to generate electricity. Tim has a lot of ideas, but Huda can see the drawbacks, or disadvantages.

Read their conversation and use ideas from it to answer the questions that follow.

Tim: Nuclear power stations can run for years without stopping – they are very reliable.

Huda: But they produce hazardous waste and they cost a lot to build.

Tim: Wind turbines are a good choice because you don't have to pay for the wind.

Huda: But they stop working when there is no wind. Many people think wind turbines are ugly.

Tim: No-one notices solar panels on the roof.

Huda: But they cost a lot and they don't work at night.

Tim: Perhaps we should use less electricity.

To evaluate the different ways of generating electricity, Tim and Huda can use three different criteria:

Reliability: Is the resource always available when we need it?

Cost: Is the resource cheap?

Effect on the environment: Does it harm the environment?

a Explain why solar electricity is unreliable.

....

....

b Explain why nuclear power is not cheap.

....

....

c Explain how wind turbines harm the environment.

....

....

2 Using your own words, write a paragraph comparing and evaluating the following energy resources:

wind   solar   nuclear

At the end of your paragraph, choose the resource you think is best for where you live. Explain the reason for your choice.

....

....

....

....

....

....

....

....

....

5 Thermal physics

This unit covers:

- ☐ the kinetic model of matter
- ☐ thermal properties of matter
- ☐ thermal (heat) energy transfers.

Exercise 5.1 Kinetic theory vocabulary

In science, we are careful to use words that everyone will understand. Scientific language is more formal than everyday language. For example, you might say, "Two particles **bump into** each other." A scientist would say, "Two atoms **collide with** each other." In this exercise, you will select scientific terms that mean the same as some everyday words and use them in sentences.

1   The list below shows some scientific words which we use when we are describing how matter behaves. For each of the sentences which follow, decide which scientific word means the same as the word in bold. Write it on the line below. The first example has been done for you.

      reflect   **inflate**   **collide with**   **evaporate**   **expand**   **diffuse**   **compress**

      A fast-moving particle will **bounce** off a smooth surface.

                                    reflect

a   A lake will **dry up** if there is no rainfall.

    ....

b   Many substances **get bigger** when they are heated.

    ....

c   Particles change direction when they **crash into** each other.

    ....

d   You can use a bicycle pump to **blow up** a flat tyre.

    ....

e It is difficult to **squash** a liquid into a smaller volume.

....

f Blue ink will **spread out** into water until the liquid is entirely blue.

....

2 Each sentence below describes something that we can explain using the kinetic model of matter. Choose a scientific word from the list on the previous page to fill the gap in each sentence.

> The words you need to fill in are all verbs. You will have to change them to the correct form to fit the sentence. For example, you might have to change *reflect* to *reflects*.

a A puddle of water .... quickly on a hot day.

b We can smell perfume because a gas .... into the air.

c The volume of a gas will decrease if you use a force to .... it.

d An iron rod .... when it is heated.

e A balloon .... as air is pumped into it.

Exercise 5.2 Explaining changes

Science is about explaining observations – things that we see. In this exercise, you will relate some observations to their scientific explanations.

Compare these two sentences:

We breathe *because* we need oxygen.

We need oxygen and *therefore* we breathe.

'We breathe' is an observation. 'We need oxygen' is the explanation – it tells us why we breathe. If we give the observation first, we use the word *because* to join it to the explanation. If we give the explanation first, we use the words *and therefore* to join it to the observation.

observation *because* explanation

explanation *and therefore* observation

1   Each of the following sentences is made up of two parts, an observation and an explanation. Complete each sentence by writing *because* or *and therefore* in the space between the two parts.

   a   Puddles of water disappear .... water evaporates into the air.

   b   Water evaporates more quickly when the temperature is high ....
   puddles disappear rapidly on a hot day.

   c   The particles of a gas move around freely .... a gas spreads out to fill
   its container.

   d   A solid has a fixed shape .... the particles of a solid have fixed positions.

   e   The particles of a liquid can move past each other .... a liquid can be
   poured from one container to another.

   f   A gas exerts pressure on its container .... the particles of a gas collide
   with the walls of its container.

2   In the space below, write two sentences which use the idea of moving particles to explain
   what happens when a liquid boils to become a gas. One sentence must include the word
   because; the other sentence must include the phrase *and therefore*.

   ....

   ....

   ....

   ....

   ....

   ....

Exercise 5.3 Instructions for calibrating a thermometer

Scientists write descriptions of their experiments so that other scientists can repeat them and
check the results. It is important that descriptions of experiments explain clearly what to do. In
this exercise, you will write instructions for how to calibrate a thermometer.

When giving instructions, we use the **imperative** form of the verb, for example:

   Dissolve salt in water.

We also use **sequencers**, that is, words that show the order in which we do things.
Sequencers are words such as *'First'*, *'Then'*, *'Next'*, *'After that'*, *'Finally'*, and so on.

The diagrams show the three stages in calibrating a liquid-in-glass thermometer. Liquid-in-glass thermometers are made from glass tubing. *Calibrating a thermometer* means adding a temperature scale to the tube.

Write instructions, based on these diagrams.

■ Make sure that your instructions are in a sensible order.

■ Each sentence should consist of one instruction only.

The first sentence has been done for you.

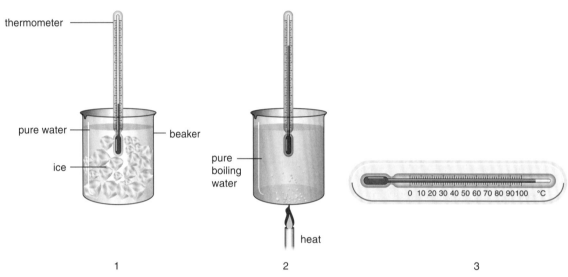

thermometer

pure water

beaker

ice

pure
boiling
water

heat

0 10 20 30 40 50 60 70 80 90 100   °C

1   2   3

1 **a** Instructions for Diagram 1

First, mix pure water and melting ice in a beaker.

....

....

....

....

....

b Instructions for Diagram 2

....

....

....

....

....

c Instructions for Diagram 3

....

....

....

....

Exercise 5.4 Thermal expansion – drawing conclusions

In science, we do experiments. We draw conclusions from our results. Then we try to explain them. In this exercise, you will select appropriate statements to describe an experiment, draw a conclusion and explain it.

The diagrams below show two stages in an experiment which demonstrates thermal expansion.

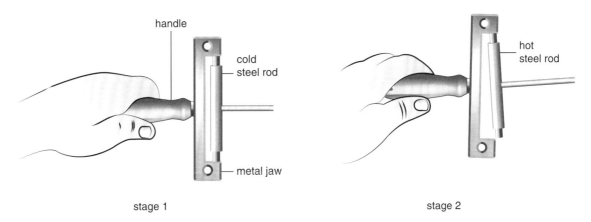

stage 1   stage 2

Below are several statements relating to this experiment.

■ Some statements *describe* the experiment.

■ Some statements are *conclusions* which might be drawn from the experiment.

■ Some statements help to *explain* the experiment.

> To *draw conclusions* means to *interpret* information. You need to make a statement about the information that you think is a fact.

1 Select some of these statements and copy them into the appropriate sections on the next page. The statements are all correct but you do not need to use all of them.

The cold steel rod fits inside the gap in the metal jaw.

All metals expand when they are heated.

The particles of a metal are farther apart when it is hotter.

The particles of a metal move faster when it is hotter.

Steel expands when it is heated.

The hot steel rod is too long to fit inside the gap in the metal jaw.

Steel is a good conductor of heat.

   a Describing the experiment

      Stage 1

      ....

      ....

      Stage 2

      ....

      ....

   b Drawing a conclusion

      ....

      ....

   c Explaining the conclusion

      ....

      ....

Exercise 5.5 Heat transfer – interpreting diagrams

Diagrams are useful because they can summarise information and ideas. In this exercise, you will interpret (draw conclusions from) three diagrams which show the three different mechanisms of thermal (heat) energy transfer.

Conduction, convection and radiation – these are the three mechanisms by which energy is transferred from a hot place to a cold place. We call these thermal energy transfers or heat energy transfers. For each of the three diagrams, state which mechanism it represents, explain how you know, and state what the arrows in the diagrams represent.

Mechanism 1

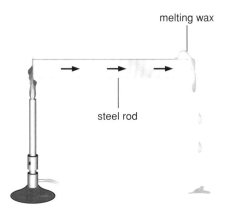

1 Which mechanism does this represent – conduction, convection or radiation?

....

2 Explain how you know.

....

....

3 What do the arrows in the diagram represent?

....

....

Mechanism 2

4 Which mechanism does this represent – conduction, convection or radiation?

....

5 Explain how you know.

....

....

6 What do the arrows in the diagram represent?

....

....

Mechanism 3

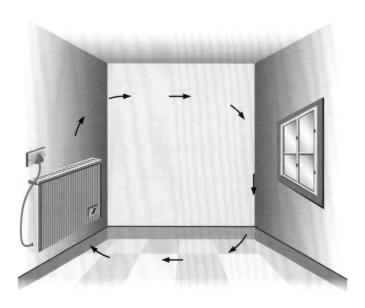

7 Which mechanism does this represent – conduction, convection or radiation?

....

8 Explain how you know.

....

....

9 What do the arrows in the diagram represent?

....

....

6 Sound and waves

This unit covers:

- ☐ how sounds are made and how they travel
- ☐ the pitch and loudness of sounds
- ☐ the properties of waves.

Exercise 6.1 Making sounds

In science, we often classify things. This means that we look at a lot of things and put them into separate classes or groups. In this exercise, you will divide up musical instruments into three classes and explain how the classes differ from each other.

1 The long line of letters below is made up of the names of nine musical instruments. Also included are the names of three classes of musical instruments. Write out the names of the instruments and the classes on the lines below. An example has been done for you.

   drum/percussion/whistlestringguitarviolintrumpetwindcymbalfluteharptambourine

Three classes of instrument:

....percussion..

Nine musical instruments:

....drum..

....

....

2 Complete the table below to show which class each instrument belongs to.

Class	Instruments
percussion	drum, ..., ...
	................................., ..., ...
	................................., ..., ...

3 All instruments in a class are played in the same way. For example:

All instruments in the percussion class are played by hitting them.

Write similar statements for the other two classes. You might need to use your dictionary, or look up some information on the internet or in reference books.

....

....

....

....

Exercise 6.2 Describing sounds

We can picture sounds as vibrations travelling through the air or through another material. In this exercise, you will define and use a number of words which are useful when we describe sounds.

1 Change the order of the letters to make words that are useful when we describe sounds.

a noibivtra ....vibration.......... **f** dioerp ....

b chpti .... **g** cyneuqref ....

c sseoulnd .... **h** dnultusaro ....

d eepsd .... **i** finsardnou ....

e muiedm .... **j** zthre ....

2 The table below contains ten definitions. Insert the correct word from question **1** next to each definition.

	Word	Definition
a		a backward and forward movement
b		how fast a sound travels
c		the solid, liquid or gas through which a sound travels
d		how loud a sound is
e		how high or low a sound is
f		the time for one complete vibration of a sound
g		the number of vibrations of a sound each second
h		the unit of frequency of a sound
i		sound which is too high-pitched to be heard
j		sound which is too low-pitched to be heard

3 Complete the following sentences by writing one of the words from the table above in each of the empty spaces.

a Sound cannot travel through a vacuum; it needs a .... to travel through.

b Blowing harder into a saxophone will increase the .... of the sound it produces.

c A sound with more vibrations each second has a higher ....

d Hz is the symbol for ....

e It is difficult to hear the sounds made by bats because they use .... to find their way around.

f The .... of sound is about 330 m/s in air.

Exercise 6.3 Oscilloscope traces

> We can use an oscilloscope to 'see' sounds as traces on a screen. In this exercise, you will write explanations of some oscilloscope traces.

1 This drawing shows a trace on an oscilloscope screen. It represents a sound wave.

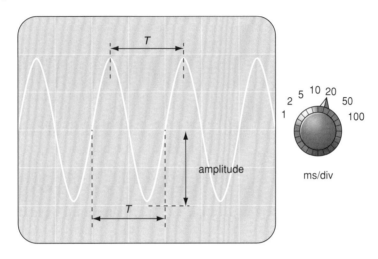

a What quantity is shown by the arrow labelled T?

....

b The vertical arrow shows the amplitude of the sound wave. Unscramble the following sentence to give a definition of 'amplitude'.

Amplitude is a maximum wave of the displacement.

....

....

You will need to use these terms in your answers to questions **2** and **3**.

2 This diagram shows two sound waves, A and B.

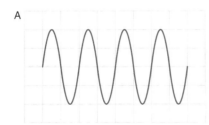
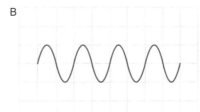

a Complete this sentence:

Sound wave A has a greater .... than sound wave B.

b If you could hear these two sounds, what difference would you notice?

....

....

3 This diagram shows two sound waves, C and D.

C

D

a Complete this sentence:

Sound wave C has a greater .... than sound wave D.

b What can you say about the frequencies of these two waves?

....

....

c If you could hear these two sounds, what difference would you notice?

....

....

Exercise 6.4 Range of hearing experiment

In this exercise, you will read a description of an experiment. You will then write a sequence of instructions which a teacher can follow to carry out the experiment.

In this experiment, the teacher can find out the highest note which any student in the class can hear. This is called the upper limit of hearing. Read this description of the experiment:

> Pupils sit with one hand up. When the pitch of the note is so high that they cannot hear it, they put their hand down. The notes come from a loudspeaker connected to a signal generator. The teacher turns the frequency control to change the pitch of the note.

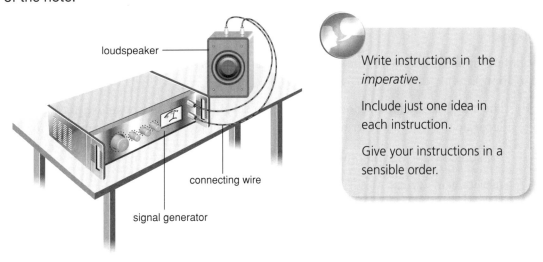

loudspeaker

connecting wire

signal generator

Write instructions in the *imperative*.

Include just one idea in each instruction.

Give your instructions in a sensible order.

On the lines below, write a series of instructions for the teacher. The first has been done for you.

First, use two wires to connect the signal generator to the loudspeaker.

....

....

....

....

....

....

....

....

Exercise 6.5 Representing waves – interpreting graphs

In this exercise, you will interpret graphs which are used to represent waves. You will also match the names of quantities to the standard symbols used to represent them.

Sound travels as a wave through air. We can represent a sound wave as a line moving up and down on a graph. Take care! There are two sorts of wave graphs:

A **displacement–distance graph** is like a photographic snapshot of a wave. It shows the displacements of the particles of the air at one moment in time. This graph shows distance on the x-axis and the displacements of the particles on the y-axis.

A **displacement–time graph** shows how a single particle of the air moves as the sound wave travels along. This graph shows time on the x-axis and the displacement of the particle on the y-axis.

(Note: **displacement** means the distance the particle has moved from its original, undisturbed position.)

1 The long line of letters below is made up of several words which we use to describe waves. Separate the words and write them on the lines below. The first has been done for you.

displacement/wavelengthtimedistanceperiodfrequencyamplitude

displacement ....

....

You will need to use these words in your answers to questions **2–5**.

2 Look at this graph.

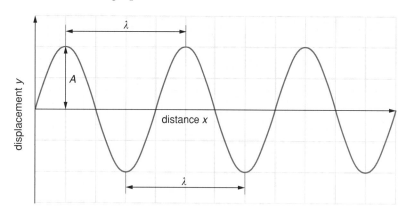

When you look at a graph, always look to see the quantities marked on the x-axis and the y-axis.

a The displacement of air particles is shown on the *y*-axis. What quantity is shown on the *x*-axis?

....

b What quantity is represented by the symbol *A*?

....

c The symbol λ is the Greek letter 'lambda'. What quantity does this represent?

....

d Which type of graph is this, a displacement–time graph or a displacement–distance graph? Explain how you can tell.

....

....

3 Look at this graph.

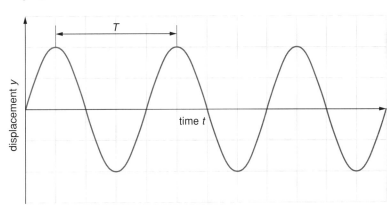

a What quantity is shown on the *x*-axis? Give the name and symbol.

....

b What quantity is shown on the *y*-axis? Give the name and symbol.

....

c What quantity is represented by the symbol *T*?

....

d Which type of graph is this, a displacement–time graph or a displacement–distance graph? Explain how you can tell.

....

....

4 Look at this graph. It represents a sound wave whose frequency is changing.

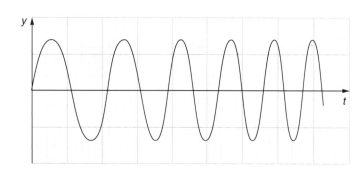

a Which type of graph is this, a displacement–time graph or a displacement–distance graph?

....

b From the graph, you can see that the height of the waves does not change. What does this tell you about the amplitude of the sound?

....

c What does this tell you about the loudness of the sound?

....

d From the graph, you can also see that the waves are becoming squashed together. The period is changing. Is it increasing or decreasing?

....

e How is the frequency of the wave changing?

....

f What would you notice if you heard this sound?

....

....

7 Light and other electromagnetic radiation

This unit covers:
- ☐ how light is reflected and refracted
- ☐ lenses and how they work
- ☐ the spectrum of visible light
- ☐ electromagnetic radiation and its uses.

Exercise 7.1 Words, symbols and definitions

A single diagram can sum up important ideas in science. However, it is important to be able to interpret scientific diagrams. In this exercise, you will complete a diagram which represents the law of reflection of light.

1 The long line of letters below is made up of six terms related to the reflection of light. Separate them out and write them on the lines below. The first has been done for you.

Take care! Several of the terms are made up of two or more words.

    mirror/incidentrayangleofincidencenormalreflectedrayangleofreflection

....mirror...

....

....

2 The table below contains definitions of four of the terms above. Choose the correct term for each definition and put it in the correct box. Complete the table by writing the remaining terms in the last two rows and adding definitions in the second column.

Term	Definition
	a ray of light travelling so that it strikes a mirror
	a smooth surface which reflects light
	the angle between an incident ray and the normal
	a line drawn at right angles to a surface where a ray of light strikes it

3 This diagram is incomplete. It illustrates the law of reflection of light. Follow the instructions to complete the diagram.

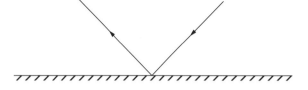

a Label the mirror.

b Label the incident ray **IR**. Explain how you know that this the incident ray.

....

....

c Label the reflected ray **RR**.

d Draw the normal to the surface of the mirror at the point where the incident ray strikes it. Mark an angle which is 90°.

e Mark the angle of incidence *i* and the angle of reflection *r*.

f We can state the law of reflection very simply, like this: $i = r$. Write this equation in words.

....

....

Exercise 7.2 Refraction of light

A ray of light may change direction when it passes from one material to another. This is refraction. In this exercise, you will describe how a ray refracts (bends) in different situations.

This diagram on the next page shows that a ray of light bends towards the normal when it travels from air into glass. This bending is called refraction. The diagram shows some important terms connected with refraction of light.

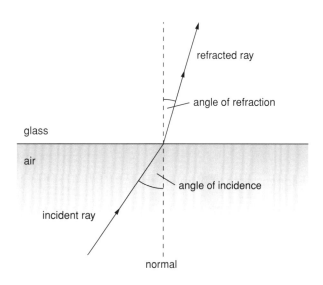

In the following questions, it may help you to draw in normal lines and to mark the angles of incidence and refraction.

1 This diagram shows a ray of light passing from water into air.

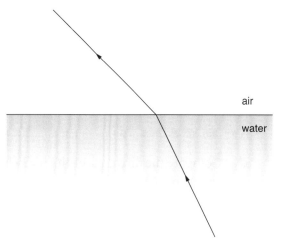

   a Does the ray of light bend towards the normal or away from the normal?

   ....

   ....

   b Which is greater, the angle of incidence or the angle of refraction?

   ....

2 This diagram shows a ray of light passing from air into plastic.

air   plastic

a Does it bend towards the normal or away from the normal?

....

....

b Which is greater, the angle of incidence or the angle of reflection?

....

3 This diagram shows a ray of light passing through a rectangular plastic block.

Use the ideas you have used in questions **1** and **2** to describe the refraction of the ray as it passes through the block.

plastic

a Describe what happens as the ray enters the block.

....

....

b Describe what happens as the ray passes through the block.

....

....

c Describe what happens as the ray leaves the block.

....

....

d Compare the direction of the ray before it enters the block with its direction after it leaves the block.

....

....

Exercise 7.3 How a lens works

Lenses have many uses. They work in a simple way: they change the directions of rays of light passing through them. If you look at an object through a lens, you will see an image of the object. In this exercise, you will practise using the vocabulary of lenses.

1 Unscramble the eight words below to make words connected with lenses and how they work.

a snel .... **e** scouf ....

b ayr .... **f** crafter ....

c gemia .... **g** lallaper ....

d grieved .... **h** greenvoc ....

2 The table below contains everyday meanings for six of the terms you have found in question **1**. Write the correct terms in the first column of the table.

	Term	Everyday meaning
a		path of a beam of light
b		in the same direction, a constant distance apart
c		bend light
d		come together
e		spread apart
f		picture made of light

3 The diagram below shows what happens when rays of light strike a converging lens. Study the diagram and answer the questions which follow. You will find the vocabulary from questions **1** and **2** useful.

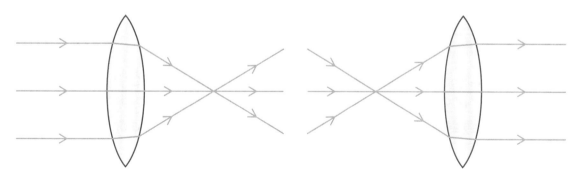

a Describe the rays before they reach the lens.

....

....

b State what happens when the rays strike the lens.

....

....

c State what happens to the rays after they have passed through the lens.

....

....

d Explain why this type of lens is called a 'converging' lens.

....

....

Exercise 7.4 The discovery of infra-red radiation

In this exercise, you will read about the discovery of infra-red radiation and answer some questions on the text that you have read.

When white light passes through a prism, it is dispersed to form a spectrum. People often use the name 'Roy G Biv' to remind them of the order of the seven colours.

1 Write the names of the seven colours on the line below, starting with 'red'.

....

....

Read the following account and answer the questions which follow.

William Herschel was an astronomer, working in England. In 1799, he decided to study the spectrum of sunlight. He thought he might learn more about the Sun.

He directed a beam of light through a prism. A spectrum formed on a piece of white paper.

Herschel knew that when sunlight is absorbed by an object, the object is warmed. He put the bulb of a thermometer in the red part of the spectrum and observed the temperature rising.

Then he made a lucky observation. As the Sun moved across the sky, the spectrum moved across the paper. Now the thermometer was no longer in the red light. It was outside the visible spectrum. Herschel was surprised to see that it showed an even higher temperature.

Herschel's deduction was that the thermometer was being warmed by invisible solar radiation. This radiation was beyond the red end of the spectrum, so he called it 'infra-red radiation'. The prefix *infra-* means *below*.

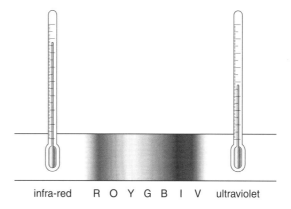

infra-red   R O Y G B I V   ultraviolet

2 Complete the first column in the table by finding words in the text which have the same meaning as the phrases in the second column. The first one has been done for you.

	Word from text	Meaning
a	astronomer	a scientist who studies the night sky
b		a triangular glass block
c		the colours of white light, arranged in order
d		the sensitive end of a thermometer
e		noticing and recording an event
f		describes light that can be detected with our eyes
g		a conclusion drawn from evidence
h		describes anything from the Sun

3 Explain why infra-red radiation is described as *invisible*.

....

....

4 a Describe Herschel's surprise observation.

....

....

b Explain why Herschel was surprised by this observation.

....

....

....

....

Exercise 7.5 The electromagnetic spectrum

In this exercise, you will write statements about the different types of radiation shown in the electromagnetic spectrum.

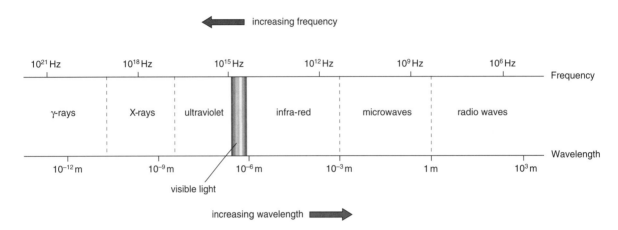

The electromagnetic spectrum shows all types of electromagnetic radiation. They are arranged in order according to their frequencies and wavelengths.

1   The statements below come in pairs. Complete the second statement of each pair using the first statement as a model.

a   Visible light lies between infra-red and ultraviolet.

Microwave radiation lies ....

....

b   Radiation with a frequency of 10^{18} Hz lies in the X-ray region of the spectrum.

Radiation with a frequency of 10^9 Hz ....

....

c   In the spectrum, wavelengths increase towards the right.

In the spectrum, frequencies increase ....

....

d   Infra-red has longer wavelengths than visible light.

Radio waves ....

....

e γ-rays have the highest frequencies in the spectrum.

Radio waves ....

....

In Exercise 1.3, we saw how to make the past simple passive. However, there are other forms of the passive that are useful in science.

One of these is the **present simple** passive. In general, we use the present simple to talk about things that are facts and/or habits. For example, 'The Sun *rises* in the east and *sets* in the west'.

To make the present simple passive, we follow the same steps we saw in Exercise 1.3. We will make this active sentence passive:

Scientists use microscopes to examine things that are too small for the eye to see.

1 First we find the object of the sentence: 'Microscopes'.

2 Next, we choose a form of the verb 'to be': in this case 'are' because 'microscopes' is plural.

3 Then, we use the past participle, or third form of the verb: 'used'.

4 Finally, we decide whether we need to include the original subject 'scientists'. In this case we do not because the function of the device is more important than who uses it.

Our passive sentence is:

Microscopes are used to examine things which are too small for the eye to see.

We can also use special verbs like 'can', 'could', 'may' and 'might' in the passive. They are called *modal verbs* because they can have several different meanings. For example;

I can understand refraction quite easily. = ability

Can I borrow your protractor? = permission

To make 'can' passive, we use *can + be + past participle*

A microscope *can be used* to see things which are too small for the eye. = possibility

2   The table below shows some uses of electromagnetic radiation.

Radiation	Used	Place
visible	to **scan** bar codes	supermarket checkout
infra-red	to **change** channels with a remote control	television
X-rays	to **provide** an image of a broken bone	hospital
microwaves	to **transmit** telephone messages	between mobile phone masts
radio waves	to **broadcast** TV programmes	transmitter
γ-rays	to **sterilise** biological equipment	laboratory

Complete the sentences below using the information in the table. In all of the sentences you will put the verbs in **bold** into the passive. Use the language box on the previous page to help you construct the sentences. You may also need to decide where to put the place listed in the third column in the sentence. Here is an example to help you:

Bar codes are scanned at the supermarket checkout using visible light.

a   The channel we are watching on television can …

....

....

b   An image of a broken bone can …

....

....

c   Telephone messages are …

....

....

d   TV programmes …

....

....

e   In a laboratory, …

....

....

8 Magnetism and static electricity

This unit covers:

☐ magnets and magnetic materials
☐ magnetic fields
☐ electromagnets
☐ static electricity and electric charge.

Exercise 8.1 Words and meanings

> In this exercise, you will define and use some scientific terms connected with magnets and magnetism.

1 The long line of letters below is made up of nine terms related to magnets and magnetism. Separate them out and write them on the lines below. The first has been done for you.

ferrous/northattractivemagnetisedsouthsoftpermanentrepulsivehard

....ferrous...

....

....

....

....

2 Now sort the terms above into groups according to their meanings. Choose the terms to match each definition.

a three words that may describe magnetic materials: ....

....

b one word that describes a piece of metal that has become a magnet: ....

c one word that describes a magnet that keeps its magnetism: ....

d two words that describe the poles of a magnet: ....

e two words that describe the forces between magnetic poles: ....

....

The terms in questions **1** and **2** are all **adjectives**. Sometimes we want to use **nouns** and **verbs** that are related to these adjectives. The table shows some of these.

Adjective	Noun	Verb
attractive	attraction	attract
repulsive	repulsion	repel
magnetised, magnetic	magnet	magnetise

3 Complete the following sentences using words from the table above. Make sure that you use the correct part of speech (adjective, noun or verb). You may also need to change the form of the verb. In question **a**, you also need to choose the correct article.

a A north pole attracts a south pole. There is a/an .... force between them.

b A north pole .... another north pole. There is a force of .... between them.

c You can make a magnet by .... a piece of iron. When it is ...., it will .... a piece of steel.

4 You can demagnetise a magnet by heating it or hammering it. *Demagnetise* is the opposite of *magnetise*. In the table below, the first column shows some verbs used in science. Complete the table by writing their opposites in the second column. The first example has been done for you.

	Verb	Opposite
a	to magnetise	to demagnetise
b	to attract	
c	to charge	
d	to contract	
e	to reflect	
f	to cool	

Exercise 8.2 Magnetic fields

In this exercise, you will use correct terminology to describe a magnetic field. You will also summarise the different ways in which the magnetic field of an electromagnet can be increased.

There is a magnetic field around a magnet. We represent the field using field lines. The field lines in this diagram represent the magnetic field around two magnets. The magnets are attracting each other. The arrows show the direction of the field.

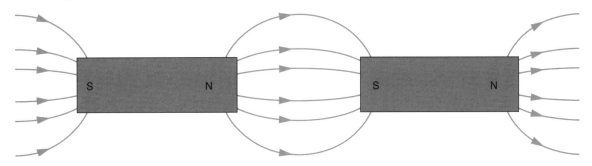

1   When describing directions, we often use **prepositions**. Use the prepositions in the list below to fill the gaps in the sentences that follow.

> A preposition is usually followed by a noun.

**to   from   towards   away from
into   out of**

a   Magnetic field lines come .... a north magnetic pole.

b   Magnetic field lines go .... a south magnetic pole.

c   A compass needle points .... the Earth's North Pole.

d   A magnet's south pole is repelled .... another magnet's south pole.

e   The electric current in an electromagnet flows .... positive .... negative.

2   An electromagnet is a coil of wire. When an electric current passes through the coil, a magnetic field is produced around it, similar to the field of a bar magnet.

Read the following paragraph which describes how the strength of the field can be changed.

> The current in the coil can be changed. If the current gets bigger, the magnetic field will be stronger. Another way to make a stronger electromagnet is to increase the number of turns of wire on the coil. A greater number of turns of wire will give a stronger magnetic field. Something else which will also have the same effect is adding an iron core. Put the core inside the coil and turn on the current. The field will be stronger because of the presence of the core.

Summarise the text by completing these three sentences:

To increase the strength of an electromagnet we can ....

....

Alternatively, we can ....

....

Thirdly, we can ....

....

Exercise 8.3 Static electricity – describing, observing and explaining

In science, we do experiments. We make observations and then we try to explain them. In this exercise, you will study an account of one experiment. Then you will write an account of another experiment.

1 The diagram below shows an experiment concerned with static electricity.

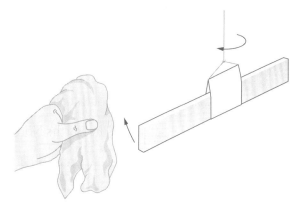

In the following account of the experiment there are three types of statements:

    Descriptions, which tell you what was done.

    Observations, which tell you what happened.

    Explanations, which tell you why it happened.

Read the account of the experiment. Read each statement in turn. Decide whether it is a description, an observation or an explanation. Beside each statement, write **D** for description, **O** for observation, or **E** for explanation.

a A plastic rod is hung using thread so that it is free to turn. ....

b One end of the rod is rubbed using a cloth. ....

c When the cloth is brought close to the rod, the rod is attracted towards the cloth. ....

d Rubbing the rod gives it a negative electric charge. ....

e The cloth is left with a positive electric charge. ....

f These opposite charges attract each other, causing the rod to move. ....

2 The picture below shows another experiment involving static electricity. Two plastic rods are charged. They repel each other.

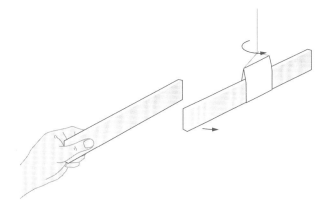

In the space below, write an account of this experiment, using the account above as a model. Your account should be in three sections: description, observation and explanation

a Description

....

....

....

....

....

b Observation

....

....

....

....

....

c Explanation

....

....

....

....

....

9 Electric circuits

This unit covers:

- ☐ conductors and insulators
- ☐ electric current and voltage
- ☐ electrical resistance
- ☐ resistors in series and parallel
- ☐ electrical safety.

Exercise 9.1 Electric current: words and meanings

When you study electric circuits, you have to learn to imagine the electric current flowing around a circuit. In this exercise, you will practise using some important words connected with electric current.

1 The long line of letters below is made up of eight terms related to electric current. Separate them out and write them on the lines below. The first has been done for you.

current/ammeterinsulatordigitalanaloguecellconductoramp

....current...

....

....

2 The table below contains definitions of the terms above. Choose the correct term for each definition and put it in the correct box. The first one has been done for you.

	Term	Definition
a	current	a flow of electric charge
b		a material that allows current to flow easily
c		a material that does not allow current to flow
d		a component which pushes a current around a circuit
e		the unit of electric current
f		a meter for measuring current
g		describes a meter with a numerical display
h		describes a meter with a needle and scale

3 Choose words from question **1** to fill the gaps in the sentences below.

a A lightning conductor is made of metal because it is a good electrical ....

b With no .... in the circuit, no charge will flow and so there will be no ....

c An electrician may wear rubber safety gloves because rubber is a good ....

d The symbol for .... is A.

Look at these two ammeters. One of these meters is analogue, the other is digital. Use the definitions from question **2** to complete the next question.

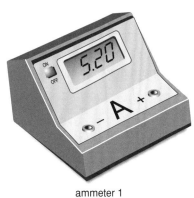

ammeter 1   ammeter 2

e Ammeter 1 is *a/an* .... meter.

Ammeter 2 is *a/an* .... meter.

f What are the readings on these ammeters?

Reading on ammeter 1 = ...

Reading on ammeter 2 = ...

> You must also choose the correct *articles* in question **e**.

Exercise 9.2 Interpreting graphs

In an electric circuit, the cell or power supply provides the potential difference (voltage) needed to make a current flow. The current depends on the resistance of the circuit. In this exercise, you will look at graphs that show how current, voltage and resistance are related. You will write sentences which describe what the graph tells us.

The resistance of an electrical component tells us how easy it is to make a current flow through it. If a bulb has a high resistance, only a small current will flow when it is connected to a cell.

A graph can sum up the relationship between two quantities. The graph on the right shows how the current through a resistor changed when the potential difference (voltage) across it was increased. To understand the graph, look at the labels on the axes:

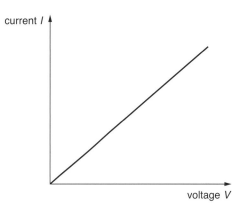

    voltage V is on the x-axis;

    current I is on the y-axis.

The graph line slopes steadily upwards, so we can say:

> The current through the resistor increased as the voltage across it increased.

The graph line passes through the origin – the point where the two axes meet. Because the graph is a straight line through the origin, we can say:

> The current through the resistor is directly proportional to the voltage across it.

Proportional means that the current increases in equal steps as the voltage is increased in equal steps.

In the questions that follow, you will study some more graphs and say what they tell you.

1   In this experiment, the resistance in the circuit was changed and the current was measured.

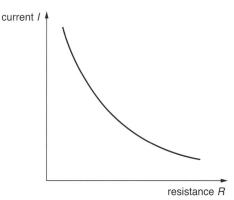

    a   Describe how the current changed as the resistance increased.

       The current increased / decreased as the resistance increased.

    b   Is the current proportional to the resistance? Explain how you know.

       Current is / is not directly proportional to the resistance. I know this because ....

       ....

2 In this experiment, wires of different lengths were connected to a cell and the current was measured.

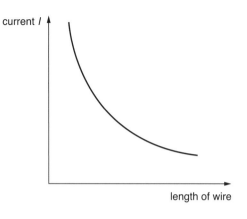

current *I*

length of wire

a Describe how the current changed as the length of the wire was increased.

The current .... as ....

....

b Which has greater resistance, a long wire or a short wire? Explain how you know.

.... has greater resistance. I know this because

....

3 In this experiment, a student compared two resistors, A and B.

a For these resistors, is the current through them proportional to the voltage across them? Explain how you know.

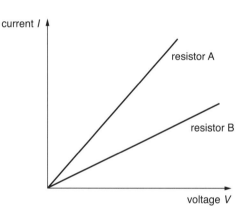

current *I*

resistor A

resistor B

voltage *V*

....

....

....

....

....

....

b Which resistor has greater resistance, A or B? Explain how you know.

....

....

....

Exercise 9.3 Describing an experiment

In science, we perform experiments to find out how two quantities are related to each other. In this exercise, you will describe an experiment that shows how the current through a resistor depends on the voltage across it.

The circuit shown below can be used to investigate how the current through a resistor depends on the voltage across it. The table shows typical results, and these have been used to draw the graph.

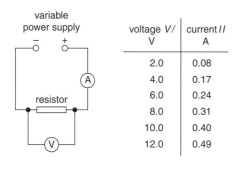

voltage V/ V	current I/ A
2.0	0.08
4.0	0.17
6.0	0.24
8.0	0.31
10.0	0.40
12.0	0.49

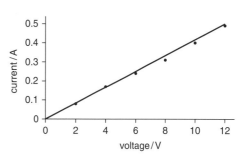

1 When writing about an experiment, it is usual to start by describing how the equipment was set up. Look at the circuit shown in the diagram. Which components would you connect together first? Then what would you do?

First, use .... to connect ....

....

.... in a series circuit.

Then, connect ....

....

....

2 Describe how you would use the circuit to get a set of results like those shown in the table. What would you change? What would you record?

Change the ....

For each value of the .... , record ....

....

3 What conclusion would you draw from the graph? (Ideas from Exercise 9.2 will help you to answer this.)

....

....

....

....

Exercise 9.4 Electrical components

In this exercise, you will read some information about thermistors and LDRs and use it to write a concise description of a thermistor.

Thermistors and light-dependent resistors (LDRs) are important components used in electric circuits. A thermistor is a resistor whose resistance changes when its temperature changes. The resistance of an LDR decreases when light shines on it. This means that these components can be used to detect changes in temperature and light level.

1 The table below includes several statements about components used in electric circuits. If a statement is a correct description of a thermistor, tick the second column. If the statement is a correct description of a light-dependent resistor (LDR), tick the third column.

thermistor   light-dependent resistor

Statement	Thermistor	LDR
resistance decreases when light falls on it		
can be used in an electronic circuit to detect light		
can be used in an electronic circuit to detect changing temperatures		
name derived from 'thermal resistor'		
resistance changes rapidly over a narrow temperature range		
can be used to switch on a heater on a cold night		
resistance given by voltage/current		
more sensitive to temperature change than an ordinary resistor		

In Exercise 2.1, we used the words 'which' and 'that' in relative clauses to give definitions. We also use the word 'whose' in relative clauses when we need a **possessive**. For example:

A resistor is a component *whose* function is to reduce or resist the flow of electricity.

Whose means the function *of* or *belonging to* the resistor. This is why it is a possessive form.

2 Use the information that you have identified in question **1** to write a paragraph which gives a concise description of a thermistor and how it can be used. You should use relative clauses in your answer that may contain 'which', 'that' and 'whose'.

A thermistor is a component ....

....

....

....

....

....

....

....

....

Exercise 9.5 Electrical safety

The mains voltage is high enough to kill you if you touch a live wire so electrical equipment must be designed to be safe to use. People are more likely to follow safety instructions if they understand the reasons for them. In this exercise, you will use your scientific understanding to explain some electrical safety features.

Compare these two sentences:

Water conducts electricity *so* you should not touch a switch with wet hands.

You should not touch a switch with wet hands *because* water conducts electricity.

'You should not touch a switch with wet hands' is a safety instruction. 'Water conducts electricity' is a scientific fact which explains the instruction. When the instruction comes first, we use the word *because* to connect it to the explanation.

instruction *because* explanation

For example, 'Don't … … because … … .'

When the explanation comes first, we use the word *so* to connect it to the instruction.

explanation *so* instruction

1 Each of the following sentences is made up of two parts, an instruction and an explanation. Complete each sentence by writing *because* or *so* in the space between the two parts.

a The mains voltage is high enough to give a fatal electric shock .... plugs must be designed to prevent the user accidentally touching any live parts.

> If something is *fatal*, it means it could kill you.

b Make sure that the metal case of an electrical appliance is earthed .... touching a live metal case could prove fatal.

c Check that the correct fuse is used .... the wrong fuse may allow an excessive current to flow.

d A circuit breaker can easily be reset .... circuit breakers should be fitted in all domestic wiring circuits.

e The case of a mains plug must be made of plastic .... plastic is an electrical insulator.

f Brass is a good conductor, which does not corrode, ... the pins of a mains plug should be made of brass.

g Do not connect more than one appliance to a socket .... the current in the wiring will be too great and this may start a fire.

2 Omar has noticed that the wiring to a fan is faulty. He sees that the insulation is damaged.

a Explain why this is dangerous.

....

....

....

b Explain what should be done to overcome this hazard.

....

....

....

3 Zola's mother has plugged several heaters into a single socket. Zola tells her mother that this could lead to the mains cables overheating.

a Explain why the cables may overheat.

....

....

....

b What could be the consequence of this overheating?

....

....

....

10 Electromagnetism

This unit covers:

- ☐ the magnetic effect of a current
- ☐ electromagnets and their uses
- ☐ electromagnetic induction
- ☐ transformers.

Exercise 10.1 Oersted's discovery

Before 1820, no-one knew about the close connection between electricity and magnetism. In this exercise, you will answer questions related to a description of the discovery of electromagnetism.

Read the following description of an experiment performed about two centuries ago, and answer the questions that follow.

> Hans Christian Oersted was a Danish scientist. He was interested in both electricity and magnetism. He gave public lectures in which he demonstrated the most recent ideas about these topics.
>
> During one lecture in 1820, he connected a long wire to a battery. As he completed the circuit, he noticed that the needle of a compass, lying on the bench, moved slightly. As a good scientist, he decided to see if he could repeat the effect. He saw that each time he completed the circuit, the needle turned. It turned back again when he broke the circuit.
>
> Oersted deduced that the current in the wire was producing a magnetic force and that this was what made the compass needle move. He placed the compass close to the wire and saw that the effect was stronger.

1 Which country did Oersted come from?

....

2 Which word in the first paragraph tells you that Oersted did experiments as well as talking about ideas?

....

3 What happens in an electric circuit when it is complete?

....

4 What happens when the circuit is broken?

....

5 In which direction does a compass needle normally point?

....

6 What effect did Oersted observe?

....

7 How did Oersted check that the effect he had observed was real?

....

8 Oersted placed the compass closer to the wire and saw that the effect was greater. What else could he have changed to produce a stronger effect?

....

....

Exercise 10.2 Making motors more powerful

An electric motor consists of an electromagnet that turns in a magnetic field. In this exercise you will label a diagram of a motor and explain how to make a more powerful motor.

The diagram shows the basic principle of an electric motor.

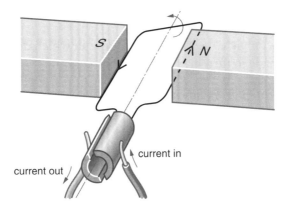

1 Add the following labels to the diagram:

permanent magnets   **coil**   **axle**   **brush**   **split-ring commutator**

2 When a current flows in the coil, it becomes magnetic. This causes the coil to be attracted by the permanent magnets, so it starts turning round. There is a *turning effect* acting on the coil.

Read the following description of how the turning effect can be changed.

> To make a motor more powerful, you need to increase the turning effect. There are several ways of doing this. For example, you can use permanent magnets that have greater strength. This will give a bigger moment. Alternatively, you can connect the motor to a higher potential difference so that a bigger current flows in the coil; again, this will increase the turning effect. You can also redesign the motor so that it has a coil with a greater number of turns of wire. Since the current feels a push each time it travels round the coil, a coil with more turns will experience a greater turning effect.
>
> You can make the coil turn the opposite way by reversing the poles of the magnets. Also, reversing the connections to the coil will make the coil rotate in the opposite direction as the current will flow the opposite way round the coil.

a The paragraph which follows describes three ways to make a motor stronger. Fill in the gaps with words from the description above – the words in brackets will give you clues.

A [*stronger*] .... motor has a greater [*moment*]

.... The strength of the motor can be increased by increasing the

[*voltage*] .... across it so that the [*amps*] ....

increases. Alternatively, you can [*change*] .... the coil so that it has

more [*coils*] .... of wire. The third way to make a motor stronger is

to use [*bar*] .... magnets which are stronger so that the

[*turning effect*] .... on the coil is greater.

b In the same way, complete the following paragraph which describes two ways in which a motor can be made to turn in the opposite direction.

In an electric motor, [*north and south*] .... poles of the magnets

face each other. By [*turning round*] .... the magnets you can make

the motor turn in the opposite [*way*] .... Alternatively, by

reversing the [*leads*] .... to the coil you will make the

[*amps*] .... flow the other way round and again the motor will turn

backwards.

Exercise 10.3 Describing an experiment

When thinking about experiments, it is important to distinguish between what is done, what is observed as a consequence and how these observations are explained. In this exercise, you will describe an experiment that shows electromagnetic induction and then explain it.

The experiment shown below is one way of demonstrating electromagnetic induction.

Read the following paragraph which describes and explains the demonstration, and answer the questions that follow. As you read the paragraph, think about three things:

- what is being done
- what is observed as a result
- how the observations are explained.

The two ends of a long electrical wire are connected to a sensitive voltmeter. Any deflection of the meter will show that a voltage has been induced in the wire. The experimenter holds a permanent magnet next to the wire. When the magnet is moved upwards next to the wire, the meter shows a reading. **However**, if the magnet is stationary, no reading is observed. Moving the magnet downwards causes a negative reading on the meter. We can picture the magnetic field lines of the magnet extending outwards from its poles. As the magnet is moved, its field lines are cut by the wire and this results in a force on the free electrons in the wire. The electrons are pushed along the wire, resulting in a current.

The linking word *'however'* is a **synonym** of *'but'*. (A synonym is a word with a similar meaning to another word.) We use *'However'*, *'Conversely'*, and *'By contrast'* when we want to contrast two opposing facts, ideas or concepts.

1 Write concise instructions for the experimental procedure. Write in short sentences, so that each sentence describes a single step in the procedure. The first sentence has been done for you.

Connect the two ends of a long electrical wire to a sensitive voltmeter.

....

....

....

....

....

2 Summarise what is observed in the experiment.

When the magnet is held stationary next to the wire, ...

....

By contrast, when the magnet is moved next to the wire, ...

....

....

....

3 Summarise the scientific explanation for these observations.

When the field lines of the magnet cut across the wire, ...

....

....

....

Conversely, when the magnet is stationary, ...

....

....

Exercise 10.4 Using transformers

In this exercise, you will describe the construction and use of transformers.

1 The diagram on the left shows the circuit symbol for a transformer. On the right is a drawing of a transformer. Label the drawing using the same labels as those that are shown on the circuit symbol.

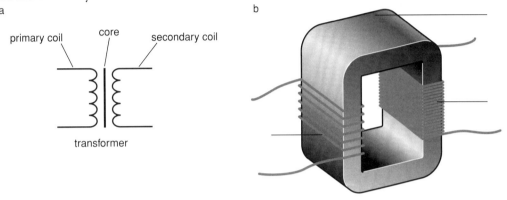

2 Complete the following sentences, choosing the correct word from each pair.

a A transformer is used to change the voltage of a supply of **alternating/direct** current.

b The transformer in the drawing is a **step-up/step-down** transformer. We know this because it has **more/fewer** turns on its secondary coil.

c If a 10 V supply is connected across the primary coil, the voltage across the secondary will be **greater/less** than 10 V.

d To connect a 12 V radio to the mains supply, a **step-up/step-down** transformer must be used because the mains voltage is **greater/less** than 12 V.

3 Transformers are used in the grid system which distributes electricity from power stations to the many users who may be several hundred kilometres from where the power is generated. This is shown in the picture below.

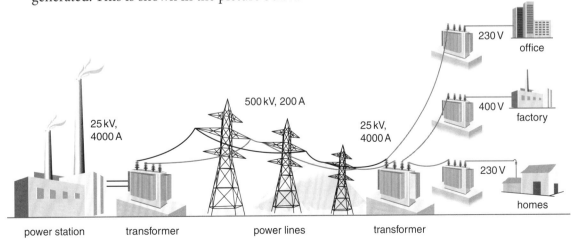

In the space below, write a paragraph to describe the grid system. You should:

- describe how the current and voltage change at different points in the grid

- explain why it is useful to increase the voltage to a high value.

You may find the following vocabulary list useful.

heating   voltage   current   reduce   increase   alternating
resistance   energy

....

....

....

....

....

....

....

....

11 Atomic physics

This unit covers:

- ☐ the structure of the atom
- ☐ nuclides and isotopes
- ☐ radioactive decay
- ☐ safe handling of radioactive materials.

Exercise 11.1 Atomic structure

In this exercise, you will interpret information about the structure of the atom presented as a diagram and as a table.

The diagram below shows a typical representation of an atom. The table contains information about the particles that make up the atom.

Study the diagram and the table and answer the questions that follow.

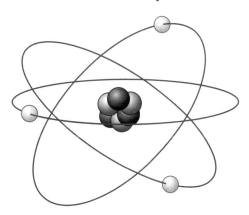

Particle	Position	Relative mass	Relative charge
proton	in nucleus	1	+1
neutron	in nucleus	1	0
electron	orbiting nucleus	1/1836	−1

1 On the diagram, label the nucleus and an electron.

2 Count the numbers of each type of particle shown in the diagram:

number of protons = ...

number of neutrons = ...

number of electrons = ...

3 Particles which are found in the nucleus are described as **nucleons**. Which two particles are nucleons?

....

4 How many nucleons are shown in the nucleus? ....

5 The word *neutral* means *having no electric charge*. Which type of nucleon is neutral?

....

6 Is the electric charge of the nucleus positive or negative? Explain how you know.

....

....

7 What force prevents the electrons from escaping from the atom?

....

8 The atom in the diagram is uncharged. Explain how you can tell this from the diagram.

....

....

9 If the atom gains or loses an electron it will become a charged **ion**. What must happen if it is to become a negatively charged ion? Explain your answer.

....

....

....

Exercise 11.2 Elements and isotopes

In this exercise, you will write and interpret symbols for various nuclides.

The diagrams below show two atoms of helium. Although both are atoms of the same element, their nuclei are different – they are different **nuclides**. Each nucleus has two protons but they have different numbers of neutrons.

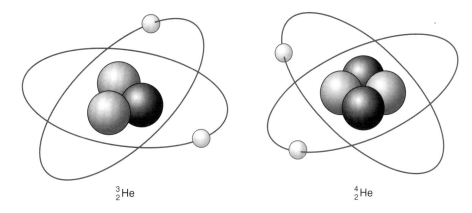

$^3_2$He $\qquad\qquad\qquad\qquad\qquad$ $^4_2$He

Each nuclide is represented by a symbol which is in three parts:

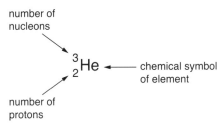

number of nucleons

$^3_2$He $\longleftarrow$ chemical symbol of element

number of protons

The prefix *super-* means 'above' or 'over'.
The prefix *sub-* means 'below' or 'under'.

1 **a** What does the subscript tell us?

  ....

  b What does the superscript tell us?

  ....

2 A particular nuclide of the element sodium is represented by the symbol $^{23}_{11}$Na.

  a What is the chemical symbol for sodium? ....

  b How many nucleons are there in this nuclide? ....

  c How many protons are there? ....

  d Calculate the number of neutrons. ....

3 An atom of nitrogen has 7 protons and 7 neutrons in its nucleus.

a How many nucleons are there in the nucleus? ....

b Write the symbol that represents this nuclide. (The chemical symbol for nitrogen is N.)

....

4 The two atoms shown at the beginning of this exercise are both atoms of helium. We know this because they have the same number of protons. However, we say that they are different *isotopes* of helium because they have different numbers of neutrons.

The table below shows the numbers of protons and neutrons in four nuclides. Which two nuclides are isotopes of the same element? Explain how you can tell.

....

....

Nuclide	Number of protons	Number of neutrons	Number of nucleons
A	12	15	27
B	13	15	28
C	13	16	29
D	14	15	29

Exercise 11.3 Background radiation

Background radiation is all around us, although we cannot see it. In this exercise, you will interpret information about background radiation presented as text and a diagram.

Read the following text, study the bar chart and answer the questions that follow.

We are all *exposed* to background radiation which we can *detect* using a Geiger counter or an electronic *sensor*. This radiation comes from radioactive substances in our *environment*. Any radiation that damages the cells of our body could *trigger* the development of cancer. Fortunately, our bodies have healing mechanisms which reduce the *risk* of this.

The greatest danger comes from radioactive substances inside our bodies. These may be in the air that we breathe or in the food and drink that we *ingest*. Once a source of radiation is inside your body there is a greater chance that its radiation will cause damage to *sensitive* tissues. At the same time, people who live at high altitudes receive a higher *dose* of radiation from cosmic rays because there is less atmosphere to *absorb* this radiation from space.

		ground and buildings 16%	food and drink 14%	cosmic rays 12%
radon and thoron gases in atmosphere 58%				

1 The paragraphs contain several words which are shown in *italics*. These words are explained in the table below. Write each word in the correct space in the first column.

	Word	**Explanation**
a		everything around us
b		to cause to begin
c		to take into our bodies
d		a device that responds to changes in the environment
e		the chance of something bad happening
f		to take in radiation so that it no longer exists
g		to record the presence of something
h		to be in the path of radiation
i		an amount of radiation received
j		describes something that responds a lot to radiation

2 Select words from the first column of the table to complete the following sentences. You may have to change the form of the word slightly.

a The crew of high-flying aircraft are exposed to higher .... of radiation from space.

b People who work with radiation may need to wear special clothing which will .... radiation. They may also wear a .... which records the amount of radiation they are exposed to.

c Rocks containing radioactive elements such as uranium will lead to higher levels of radiation in the ....

d A Geiger counter is .... enough to detect the radioactive decay of a single atom.

e Although there is a .... that background radiation may harm us, most people are not harmed by it during their lifetimes.

3 A doctor sees a patient who has a persistent cough. The doctor recommends that the patient should have a chest X-ray to be sure there is no serious lung disease. However, this will increase the patient's annual dose of radiation by 10%.

Explain why it is a good idea for the patient to be X-rayed even though this will increase their exposure to radiation.

....

....

....

....

....

....

....

....

....

Exercise 11.4 Alpha, beta, gamma

> In this exercise, you will use information contained in diagrams to complete sentences which compare the three different types of radiation given out by radioactive substances.

Some atoms are described as radioactive. This means that they have an unstable nucleus, which decays by emitting radiation. There are three types of radiation emitted by radioactive atoms. We call them alpha, beta and gamma, the first three letters of the Greek alphabet. Here are their symbols:

alpha α

beta β

gamma γ

The diagram on the top of the next page shows the three different types of radiation. The diagram on the bottom shows which materials can absorb each type of radiation.

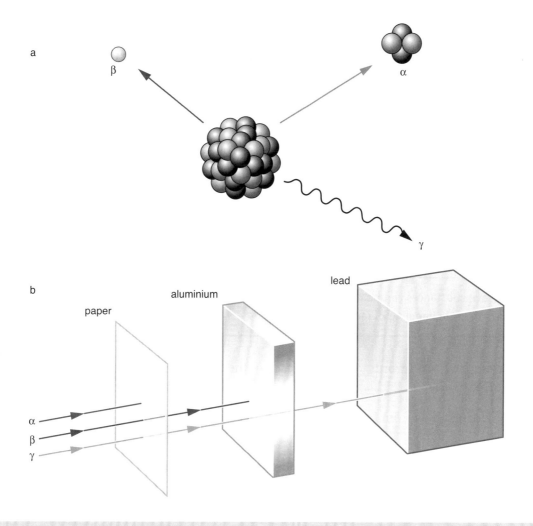

a

b

As we saw in Exercise 3.1, if we want to describe how two things differ, we may write two sentences joined by the word 'but', 'while' or 'whereas'.

We can also use the linking words that we saw in Exercise 10.3 to make a contrast.

Complete each of the following statements. You will find the information you need in the two diagrams above.

1 Alpha and beta radiations are particles while gamma radiation is ....

....

2 Alpha radiation has a positive charge whereas beta radiation ....

....

3 Alpha and beta radiations are electrically charged. By contrast, gamma radiation ....

....

4   Gamma radiation can pass through aluminium but beta radiation ....

....

5   Alpha radiation is absorbed by paper. However, gamma radiation ....

....

6   Gamma radiation is very penetrating. Conversely, alpha radiation ....

....

Exercise 11.5 Handling radioactive substances

Radioactive substances can be dangerous. In this exercise, you will complete sentences which describe the safe handling of radioactive substances.

1   Choose the correct words to complete each of the following sentences. Cross out the incorrect words.

    a   The radiation from radioactive substances can be hazardous/penetrating because it can damage living cells.

    b   A radioactive substance decays/emits radiation all the time.

    c   When handling a radioactive substance you should wear rubber gloves to avoid being contaminated/irradiated by the substance.

    d   A radioactive source should be stored in a lead box because lead deflects/absorbs radiation.

    e   Radiation is described as 'ionising' because it causes cells/atoms to become electrically charged.

    f   Radiation spreads out in all directions from a source, which means that it is weaker/stronger the further away you are from the source.

2 Some radioactive sources are handled using long tongs, as shown below.

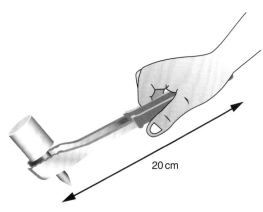

20 cm

a Explain how this helps the user to avoid being contaminated by the radioactive substance.

....

....

....

b Explain why using tongs means that the user is irradiated less.

....

....

....

Answer key

1 Making measurements

Exercise 1.1 Quantities and how they are measured

1 a length, ruler, 22.4 cm
   b cm (centimetre)

2 a, b

Measuring instrument	Quantity measured	Unit
ruler	length	metre
measuring cylinder	volume	metre cubed
clock	time	second
thermometer	temperature	degree Celsius

You might have written other units such as

– *length in centimetres, kilometres, miles or feet*
– *volume in centimetres cubed, litres or millilitres*
– *time in hours, days or years*
– *temperature in degrees Fahrenheit.*

All of those, and many others, would be correct. Remember that in science we use SI units, based on the metre, kilogram and second.

   c A measuring cylinder is used to measure volume in metres cubed.

     A clock is used to measure time in seconds.

     A thermometer is used to measure temperature in degrees Celsius.

If you chose different units in question 2b, your sentences will look a little different. Make sure the structure of your sentences is the same as the ones shown here.

3 *Your paragraph should look something like this:*

First, we half-filled a measuring cylinder with water. Then, we recorded the volume. Next, to determine the volume of the pebble, we immersed it in the water. After that, we recorded the new volume. Finally, we calculated the volume of the pebble from the difference between the two volumes.

You might have used the structuring words 'Then', 'Next' and 'After that' in a different order.

Exercise 1.2 Quantities and units

1 30 °C, 5 km, 2 h, 1.5 dm^3, 10 kg

2

Quantity	Value	Unit
temperature	30	degree Celsius (°C)
distance	*5*	*kilometre (km)*
time	*2*	*hour (h)*
volume	*1.5*	*litre (l)*
mass	*10*	*kilogram (kg)*

3 a centi-
   b metre
   c milli-
   d millimetre

e *For example:* g (gram), kg (kilogram); *in science, we do not use other units such as pounds and ounces.*

f *For example:* mm (millimetre), cm (centimetre); *in science, we do not use other units such as miles and inches.*

g millisecond

h 1 ms; *1 μs is one microsecond, which is one millionth of a second. It is a thousand times smaller than a millisecond, which is one thousandth of a second.*

i volume

Exercise 1.3 Measuring density

1 **a** The density of water is 1000 kilograms per metre cubed.

b density of water = 1 kg/dm^3

c mass

d volume

e density = mass / volume

2 **a** heavy, heavier, heaviest

b high, higher, highest

c low, lower, lowest

d dense, denser, densest.

3 **a** lead

b denser

c aluminium

d lower

e aluminium

f *For example:* The density of silver is less than the density of gold. Gold is denser than silver. Platinum is the densest of the three metals.

4 Next, we recorded the volume of the water. Then we weighed the cylinder to find its mass. We immersed the steel in the water and recorded the volume of the water again. Finally, we weighed the cylinder again.

5 Next, the volume of the water was recorded. Then the cylinder was weighed to find its mass. The steel was immersed in the water and the volume of the water was recorded again. Finally, the cylinder was weighed again.

2 Describing motion

Exercise 2.1 Movement – word definitions

1 speed; distance; motion; decelerate; metre; gradient; calculate; equation; accelerate

2 **a** equation

b calculate

c gradient

d metre

e distance

f speed

g decelerate

h accelerate

i motion

Exercise 2.2 Interpreting the shape of a graph

1 is greater (steeper); at greater speed (faster, more quickly)

2 is zero (horizontal, flat); stationary (not moving)

Exercise 2.3 Making comparisons

1 Amrita 6.0 m/s; Nailan 8.0 m/s; Surriya 6.7 m/s

2 **a** shorter

b correct

c shorter

d longest

e lower

f correct, lowest

Exercise 2.4 Changing speed

1

Description	Constant speed	Accelerating	Decelerating
moving at a steady speed	✔		
going faster		✔	
slowing down			✔
travelling at 30 m/s	✔		
speeding up		✔	
coming to a halt			✔
increasing speed		✔	
changing speed from 40 m/s to 20 m/s			✔
travelling 25 m each second	✔		

2 A The car is going faster / speeding up / accelerating

B The car is moving at a steady speed / constant speed / is travelling 25 m each second

C The car is slowing down / decelerating

D The car is moving at a steady speed / constant speed

E The car is slowing down / decelerating / coming to a halt

Exercise 2.5 Acceleration – interpreting questions

1 a change of speed (how much its speed increases)

b change in speed is 80 km/h – 0 km/h = 80 km/h

2 a acceleration (rate at which speed is increasing)

b change of speed = 16 – 4 = 12 m/s
acceleration = 12 / 4.8 = 2.5 m/s^2

3 a change in speed (how fast)

b change in speed = 10 × 3.5 = 35 m/s

4 a time (how long)

b time = 10 / 1.6 = 6.25 s

Exercise 2.6 A journey by coach

1, 2

Section	Clock time at end	Time taken / hours	Distance travelled / km	Average speed / km/h
bus station to edge of town	13:30	0.5	5	5 / 0.5 = 10
motorway	14:30	1.0	85	85
country road	14:50	0.33	15	45
village square	15:00	0.16	0	0

3 *See graph*

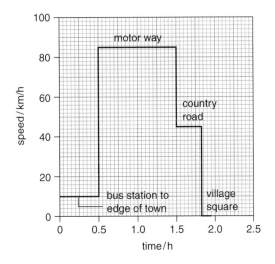

3 The effects of forces

Exercise 3.1 Mass and weight

1

Statement	Mass	Weight
... is a force		✔
... is the pull of the Earth's gravity on an object		✔
... has the symbol *m*	✔	
... is the amount of matter something is made of	✔	
... has a direction		✔
... is measured in kilograms	✔	
... is measured in newtons		✔
... can be represented by an arrow		✔
... decreases when an object travels out into space		✔

2   Mass is the amount of matter something is made of.

Weight is the pull of the Earth's gravity on an object.

3 **a**   but/while/whereas your weight decreases.

   b   but/while/whereas weight is measured in newtons.

4 **a**   mark at highest point
   b   mark at sixth image from top
   c   ... the gaps between the images increase. This shows that, in each interval of 0.1 s, the ball falls a greater distance. This shows that its speed is increasing.

Exercise 3.2 Moments and stability

1 a important / significant / historic *or something similar*
b huge / enormous / very big *or something similar*
c unsteady / wobbly *or something similar*

2 moment, mass, stable

3

Physics word	Definition
mass	the amount of matter in an object
moment	the turning effect of a force
stable	describes an object which will not easily fall over

4 a it acts further from the pivot.
b its centre of mass is lower.

Exercise 3.3 Stretching springs

1 a exert a force on …. become deformed
b compressed
c extends
d increasing the force … deformation

2 a extend
b compress
c deform
d increase

3

Length	Symbol
original length	l
final length	L
extension	x

4 Statements **a**, **b**, **d**, **e**, **f** and **g** are correct.
Statement **c** is incorrect.

5 a

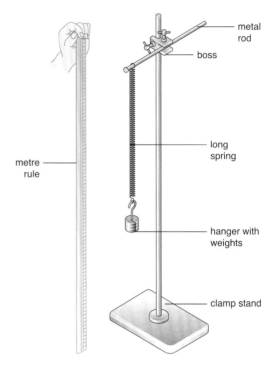

b Hang the spring from the rod.

Measure the length of the spring.

Attach the hanger to the end of the spring.

Measure the length of the spring again.

Add a weight to the hanger.

Measure the spring again.

Repeat, adding weights and measuring the length each time.

Exercise 3.4 Pressure

1 *For example:* force, weight, area, pressure, fluids, barometer

2 a pressure
b weight
c fluid
d atmospheric pressure
e barometer

3 *For example*:

a If Alok stands on the roof, the pressure will be high because the force of his weight is pressing on a small area. The high pressure will break the roof.

b If Alok crawls on a plank, the force of his weight will be pressing on a much bigger area and so the pressure will be less.

4 Energy and work

Exercise 4.1 Recognising forms of energy

1 kinetic; thermal; chemical; strain; light; sound; nuclear; internal; electrical; gravitational potential

2 **a** chemical energy
b internal energy
c gravitational potential energy
d electrical energy
e nuclear energy

3 **a** Kinetic energy:

A bus is travelling along a road. It is moving. Therefore it is a store of kinetic energy.

b Chemical energy:

Many people use coal as a fuel. Its energy is released when it burns. Burning is a chemical reaction. Therefore it is a store of chemical energy

4 *Strain energy is stored in objects that are stretched or squashed in an elastic way. A force has been used to deform the object, and when it is released the object will return to its original shape. The stored*

energy can be given to other objects when it is released. Your answer should cover these points. It might look something like this:

A force can be used to stretch a rubber band. A stretched band can be used fire a paper pellet. The pellet is given energy by the band. Therefore the stretched band is a store of strain energy.

Exercise 4.2 Energy transfers

1 **a** Energy that we can see with our eyes *is called light* energy.
b Energy that is being transferred in an electric circuit *is called electrical* energy.
c Energy that is transferred when a force pushes an object *is called work*.
d Energy that is spreading out from a hot object *is called heat* energy and *thermal* energy.

2 **a**

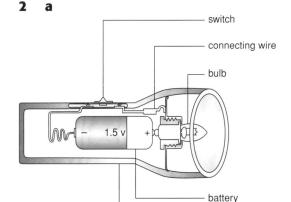

b The energy is stored as chemical energy in the battery.
c Energy is transferred from the battery to the bulb as electrical energy in the wires. In the bulb, electrical energy is transformed to light energy and heat energy.

Exercise 4.3 Where we get our energy from

1 a *correct*
b *incorrect*; We use **less** gas than coal.
c *incorrect*; We use **half** as much hydro as nuclear. / We use **twice** as much nuclear as hydro.

2 *For example:*
a We use less biomass than gas.
b We use more gas than biomass.
c We use twice as much nuclear as hydro.
d We use oil the most.
e We use other renewables the least.

Exercise 4.4 Energy resources

1 a Solar electricity is not available at night (when the Sun isn't shining).
b Nuclear power stations are expensive to build and their hazardous waste must be stored.
c Wind turbines are ugly (according to some people).

2 *Your paragraph should refer to the three energy resources and to their reliability, cost and effect on the environment. When you choose which energy resource you think is best, you must give reasons.*

5 Thermal physics

Exercise 5.1 Kinetic theory vocabulary

1 a evaporate
b expand
c collide with
d inflate
e compress
f diffuse

2 a evaporates
b diffuses
c compress
d expands
e inflates

Exercise 5.2 Explaining changes

1 a because
b and therefore
c and therefore
d because
e and therefore
f because

2 *For example:*

At high temperatures, a liquid becomes a gas because its particles break free of each other.

At high temperatures, the particles of a liquid break free of each other so the liquid becomes a gas.

Exercise 5.3 Instructions for calibrating a thermometer

Here are suggested answers. Your sentences may be slightly different, and you may have used the sequencers (first, next, after that, finally) in different places.

1 a First, put the bulb of the thermometer in the mixture.

When the reading is constant, mark the level of liquid.

b Next, put pure water in a beaker.

Heat the water until it boils.

Put the bulb of the thermometer in the water.

When the reading is constant, mark the level of liquid.

c After that, label the two marks as 0 °C and 100 °C.

Measure the distance along the thermometer between the two marks.

Calculate the distance represented by 10 °C.

Divide the scale between 0 and 100 into 10 equal parts.

Finally, divide each division into 10 smaller divisions.

Exercise 5.4 Thermal expansion – drawing conclusions

1 **a** Stage 1: The cold steel rod fits inside the gap in the metal jaw.

Stage 2: The hot steel rod is too long to fit inside the gap in the metal jaw.

b Drawing a conclusion: Steel expands when it is heated.

c Explaining the conclusion: The particles of a metal are farther apart when it is hotter.

Exercise 5.5 Heat transfer – interpreting diagrams

Mechanism 1
1 conduction
2 It is happening in a solid.
3 Energy conducting along the steel rod

Mechanism 2
4 radiation
5 Energy is spreading out from a hot source.
6 Energy radiating outwards (infra-red radiation)

Mechanism 3
7 convection
8 Air (a fluid) is moving, carrying energy with it.
9 Movement of warm air (upwards) and cold air (downwards)

6 Sound and waves

Exercise 6.1 Making sounds

1 percussion, string, wind

drum, whistle, guitar, violin, trumpet, cymbal, flute, harp, tambourine

2

Class	Instruments
percussion	drum, *cymbal, tambourine*
string	*guitar*, *violin*, *harp*
wind	*whistle*, *trumpet*, *flute*

3 All instruments in the string class are played by making the strings vibrate (by plucking or using a bow).

All instruments in the wind class are played by blowing them.

Exercise 6.2 Describing sounds

1 **a** vibration
b pitch
c loudness
d speed
e medium
f period
g frequency
h ultrasound
i infrasound
j hertz

2
 a vibration
 b speed
 c medium
 d loudness
 e pitch
 f period
 g frequency
 h hertz
 i ultrasound
 j infrasound

3
 a medium
 b loudness
 c frequency
 d hertz
 e ultrasound
 f speed

Exercise 6.3 Oscilloscope traces

1 **a** period
  b Amplitude is the maximum displacement of a wave.

2 **a** amplitude
  b A is louder than B.

3 **a** period
  b D has a greater frequency than C.
  c D has a higher pitch than C.

Exercise 6.4 Range of hearing experiment

Switch on the signal generator.

Set it to a low frequency so that the class can hear the sound.

Ask the class to put their hands up.

Tell the class to put their hands down when they can no longer hear the sound.

Slowly increase the frequency.

Note the frequency at which the last student's hand is lowered.

Exercise 6.5 Representing waves – interpreting graphs

1 wavelength, time, distance, period, frequency, amplitude

2 **a** distance
  b amplitude
  c wavelength
  d displacement–distance; because distance x is on the x-axis.

3 **a** time t
  b displacement y
  c period
  d displacement–time; because time t is on the x-axis.

4 **a** displacement–time
  b The amplitude of the sound is constant.
  c The loudness of the sound is constant.
  d The period is decreasing.
  e The frequency is increasing.
  f The pitch is increasing. (*or* The sound is getting higher.)

7 Light and other electromagnetic radiation

Exercise 7.1 Words, symbols and definitions

1 incident ray; angle of incidence; normal; reflected ray; angle of reflection

2

Term	Definition
incident ray	a ray of light travelling so that it strikes a mirror
mirror	a smooth surface which reflects light
angle of incidence	the angle between an incident ray and the normal
normal	a line drawn at right angles to a surface where a ray of light strikes it
reflected ray	*a ray of light after it is reflected by a mirror*
angle of reflection	*the angle between a reflected ray and the normal*

3   a, c–e   *see diagram*

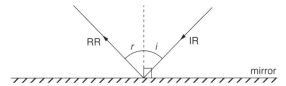

    b   This is the ray that strikes the mirror.

    f   The angle of incidence equals the angle of reflection.

Exercise 7.2 Refraction of light

1   a   The ray of light bends away from the normal.

    b   The angle of refraction is greater.

2   a   The ray of light bends towards the normal.

    b   The angle of incidence is greater.

3   a   As the ray enters the block, it bends towards the normal.

    b   The ray remains straight as it passes through the block.

    c   As it leaves the block, it bends away from the normal.

    d   After the ray leaves the block, it is travelling in the same direction as it was before it entered the block. (*or* The ray is parallel to the ray before it entered the block.)

Exercise 7.3 How a lens works

1   a   lens
    b   ray
    c   image
    d   diverge
    e   focus
    f   refract
    g   parallel
    h   converge

2   a   ray
    b   parallel
    c   refract
    d   converge
    e   diverge
    f   image

3   a   The rays are parallel.
    b   The rays are refracted.
    c   The rays meet at one point, the focus (and then spread out).
    d   Parallel rays are made to converge by a converging lens.

Exercise 7.4 The discovery of infra-red radiation

1   Red, orange, yellow, green, blue, indigo, violet

2   a   astronomer
    b   prism
    c   spectrum
    d   bulb
    e   observation
    f   visible
    g   deduction
    h   solar

3   *Invisible* means that it cannot be seen by the human eye.

4 **a** The temperature recorded by the thermometer was higher beyond the red end of the spectrum.

    b Herschel did not know that there was any radiation beyond the red end of the spectrum so he thought the temperature would be lower there.

Exercise 7.5 The electromagnetic spectrum

1 **a** Microwave radiation lies between infra-red and radio waves.

    b Radiation with a frequency of 10^9 Hz lies in the microwaves region of the spectrum.

    c In the spectrum, frequencies increase towards the left.

    d Radio waves have longer wavelengths than microwaves.

        Radio waves have longer wavelengths than visible light.

        Radio waves have lower frequencies than visible light.

        Note that you have to use 'have' because 'radio waves' is plural. The model statement uses 'has' because the subject 'Infra-red' is singular.

    e Radio waves have the lowest frequencies in the spectrum.

2 *Note that we use the passive form of the verb in these answers:*

    a The channel we are watching on television can **be changed with a remote control using infra-red radiation**.

    b An image of a broken bone can **be provided in a hospital using X-rays**.

    c Telephone messages are **transmitted between mobile phone masts using microwaves**.

    d TV programmes **are broadcast by a transmitter using radio waves**.

    e In a laboratory, **biological equipment is sterilised using gamma rays**.

8 Magnetism and static electricity

Exercise 8.1 Words and meanings

1 ferrous, north, attractive, magnetised, south, soft, permanent, repulsive, hard

2 **a** ferrous, hard, soft
    b magnetised
    c permanent
    d north, south
    e attractive, repulsive

3 **a** an attractive
    b repels; repulsion
    c magnetising; magnetised; attract

4 **a** to demagnetise
    b to repel
    c to discharge
    d to expand / to extend
    e to absorb
    f to heat

Exercise 8.2 Magnetic fields

1 **a** out of (*or* from *or* away from)
    b into (*or* towards)
    c towards (*or* to)
    d away from (*or* from)
    e from, to

2 *You can have these answers in any order:*

    increase the current.

    increase the number of turns of wire.

    put an iron core inside the coil.

Exercise 8.3 Static electricity – describing, observing and explaining

1 **a** D
   b D
   c O
   d E
   e E
   f E

2 **a** Description:

   A plastic rod is hung so that it is free to turn.

   The rod and a second rod are rubbed with a cloth.

   The second rod is brought close to the first.

   b Observation:

   The hanging rod moves round as the other rod is brought close.

   c Explanation:

   Rubbing the cloths gives them both an electric charge.

   They both have charge of the same sign.

   There is a repulsive force between the rods because like charges repel.

9 Electric circuits

Exercise 9.1 Electric current: words and meanings

1 current, ammeter, insulator, digital, analogue, cell, conductor, amp

2 **a** current
   b conductor
   c insulator
   d cell
   e amp
   f ammeter
   g digital
   h analogue

3 **a** conductor
   b cell; current
   c insulator
   d amp
   e a digital; an analogue
   f 5.20 A; 4.0 A

Exercise 9.2 Interpreting graphs

1 **a** The current **decreased** as the resistance increased.
   b Current **is not** proportional to the resistance. I know this because **the graph is not a straight line through the origin**.

2 **a** The current **decreased** as **the length of the wire increased**.
   b **A long wire** has greater resistance. I know this because **it allows less current to flow**. (*or equivalent*)

3 **a** Current is proportional to voltage. I know this because the graphs are straight lines through the origin.
   b Resistor B has greater resistance. I know this because it lets less current through than resistor A. (*or equivalent*)

Exercise 9.3 Describing an experiment

1 First, use **connecting wires** to connect **the variable power supply, the resistor and the ammeter** in a series circuit.

   Then, connect **the voltmeter in parallel with the resistor**.

2 Change the *variable power supply*.

For each value of the *voltage*, record *the voltage and the current*.

3 The graph is a straight line through the origin. This shows that the current is proportional to the voltage.

Exercise 9.4 Electrical components

1

Statement	Thermistor	LDR
resistance decreases when light falls on it		✔
can be used in an electronic circuit to detect light		✔
can be used in an electronic circuit to detect changing temperatures	✔	
name derived from 'thermal resistor'	✔	
resistance changes rapidly over a narrow temperature range	✔	
can be used to switch on a heater on a cold night	✔	
resistance given by voltage / current	✔	✔
more sensitive to temperature change than an ordinary resistor	✔	

2 *For example*:

A thermistor is a component whose name is derived from 'thermal resistor'. It is a resistor whose resistance changes rapidly over a narrow temperature range. This makes it more sensitive to temperature change than an ordinary resistor, so it can be used in an electronic circuit to switch on a heater on a cold night.

Exercise 9.5 Electrical safety

1 a so
  b because
  c because
  d so
  e because
  f so
  g because

2 a The metal wires may be exposed. Someone touching them could get an electric shock.

  b The wiring should be replaced. (*or* Insulating tape could be used to replace the insulation.)

3 a With several heaters connected, the current may be too great. A big current will heat the wires.

  b A fire may start. (*or* The insulation of the wires may catch fire.)

10 Electromagnetism

Exercise 10.1 Oersted's discovery

1 Denmark

2 demonstrated

3 A current flows.

4 The current stops.

5 To the north. (*or* north–south)

6 The needle changed direction when the current flowed.

7 He repeated his observation.

8 He could have increased the current.

Exercise 10.2 Making motors more powerful

1

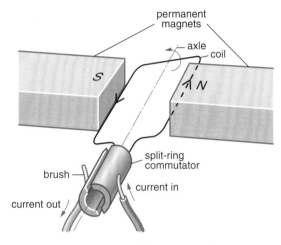

2 a more powerful, turning effect, potential difference, current, redesign, turns, permanent, moment

b opposite, reversing, direction, connections, current

Exercise 10.3 Describing an experiment

1 Connect the two ends of a long electrical wire to a sensitive voltmeter.

Hold the magnet so that one pole is close to the wire.

Move the magnet upwards past the wire.

Hold the magnet stationary next to the wire.

Move the magnet downwards past the wire.

2 When the magnet is held stationary next to the wire, *no reading is seen on the voltmeter*.

By contrast, when the magnet is moved next to the wire, *a reading is seen on the voltmeter. Moving the magnet in the opposite direction produces a negative reading.*

3 When the field lines of the magnet cut across the wire, *there is a force on the electrons in the wire. This makes a current flow in the wire.*

Conversely, when the magnet is stationary, *there is no force on the electrons and so there is no current*.

Exercise 10.4 Using transformers

1

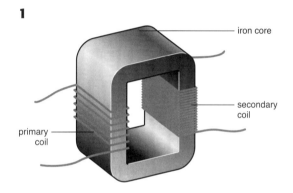

2 a alternating
b step-up, more
c greater
d step-down, greater

3 *Look at the diagram step-by-step, starting from the left. Describe each section in turn. Include words or phrases that show when you are explaining, rather than simply describing ('this means that', 'and so'). For example:*

A power station produces alternating current. The voltage is typically 25 kV. A step-up transformer is used to increase this to 500 kV. This means that the current in the power lines is reduced and so less energy is wasted as heat because of the resistance of the cables. Step-down transformers are used to reduce the voltage to a suitable level for use in factories, offices and homes.

11 Atomic physics

Exercise 11.1 Atomic structure

1 *nucleus – the structure at the centre of the diagram*

electron – any of the three spheres at the edge of the diagram

2 3, 3, 3

3 protons and neutrons

4 6

5 neutron

6 Positive, because protons are positive and neutrons are neutral.

7 Electric force of attraction between positive and negative charges (protons and electrons).

8 The positive charge of three protons is balanced by the negative charge of three electrons.

9 It must gain an electron – this adds negative charge to the atom.

Exercise 11.2 Elements and isotopes

1 a the number of protons in the nucleus
b the number of nucleons in the nucleus

2 a Na
b 23
c 11
d $23 - 11 = 12$

3 a 14
b $^{14}_{7}\text{N}$

4 B and C, because they have the same number of protons.

Exercise 11.3 Background radiation

1 a environment
b trigger
c ingest
d sensor
e risk
f absorb
g detect
h exposed
i dose
j sensitive

2 a doses
b absorb, sensor
c environment
d sensitive
e risk

3 *For example:*

The X-ray may show a problem which can then be treated. Without the X-ray, the problem could get worse. Although the X-ray increases the patient's dose of radiation, there is only a small risk that this will cause health problems such as cancer.

Exercise 11.4 Alpha, beta, gamma

1 electromagnetic radiation

2 has a negative charge

3 is neutral/uncharged

4 is absorbed by aluminium / can only pass through paper

5 passes through paper / is not absorbed / is transmitted

6 is easily absorbed / is not very penetrating

Exercise 11.5 Handling radioactive substances

1 **a** hazardous *(Radiation is penetrating, but this is not because it can damage living cells.)*
   b emits radiation
   c contaminated *(Gloves cannot stop radiation completely, but they will prevent the dangerous material from sticking to your skin.)*
   d absorbs
   e atoms *(An atom becomes ionised when radiation knocks an electron off it.)*
   f weaker

2 **a** *For example*:

   The user will not be in direct contact with the radioactive source. None of the radioactive material can reach their skin.

   b *For example*:

   The user's hand is further from the radioactive source. If they held the source, they would be closer to it. They would receive a bigger dose of radiation because the radiation is stronger near to the source.

Language file

1 Types of word

1.1 Verbs

Verb forms

All verbs have three basic forms:

- the base form
- the past form
- the past participle form.

Many verbs are regular. Their past and past participle forms end in '-ed'.

For example: heat, heated, heated

There are also many irregular verbs.

For example: rise, rose, risen

We just have to learn these irregular verbs.

1   The base form
    The base form of a verb has three main uses. We use this form in the present simple tense to talk about things which are true. For example, 'I like physics'. If we use the subjects he/she/it in the present simple, we must add 's'. For example, 'She likes physics'.

    We can also use the base form as an infinitive or imperative – see below for more information about how the infinitive is used.

2   The past form
    We can use the past form of the verb to talk about activities that started and finished in the past. We often say when the activity happened. For example, 'Newton discovered the law of gravity in the 17th century'.

3   The past participle form
    In science, the past participle form is mostly used when we want to make an active sentence passive. Go to Exercise 1.3 for more information about this.

Imperatives

Imperatives are verbs used to give instructions, orders or commands. They are used in the base or infinitive form.

For example: *Measure* the amount of carbon dioxide produced.

Evaluate how well you did the experiment.

Calculate your body mass index.

Command verbs

In tests and exams, you are given instructions as to what you should do. Below are the most common command verbs used in exams. Make sure you know what each word means, as it will help you to answer questions correctly.

Calculate	Perform a mathematical operation to find a numerical answer. You will usually need to show your working.
Compare	Say what is the same and what is different about two or more things.
Complete	Label a diagram or fill in gaps in a text or table.
Deduce	Give an answer based on information in the question.
Define	Give a precise description of the meaning of a term. Do not add any explanations.
Describe	Say what you can see in a graph, diagram or table. *or*
	Give the steps of what happens in a process.
	You do not need to give any explanation.
Discuss	Give two or more sides of an argument.
Draw	Provide a diagram, graph etc.
Estimate	State about how much or how many. This might involve a calculation using approximate values.
Explain	You need to give reasons in your answer. Often you will need to explain why something happens, or why a process is used.
Find	Calculate, measure or otherwise determine the answer.
Interpret	Use data to draw conclusions.
List	Give a number of (usually short) points. Often the number of points required is stated in the question.
Measure	Use a measuring instrument (for example ruler, calipers) to find a quantity.
Name/label	Add names or labels to a diagram
Outline	Give the main points of a topic or process as briefly as you can.
Predict	Say what you think will happen, based on the information in the question.
Refer to	Use information given as part of the question in your answer.
Show that	Give the steps of how you reached an answer.
Sketch	Provide a rough drawing; not a precise one.
Solve	Find the answer.
State	Give a short answer with no explanation, usually just simple facts. Sometimes you will be able to take the answer directly from the question.
Suggest	This could mean you need to give some of your own ideas, or to give one possible answer when there is more than one correct answer.

1.2 Articles

Using 'a', 'an' and 'the'

The form of 'a' or 'an' depends on the word (noun or adjective) that follows it.

If the next word begins with a consonant, use 'a':   *A digital meter displays a numerical value.*

If the next word begins with a vowel (a, e, i, o, u), use 'an':   *An analogue meter has a scale.*

You use 'a' or 'an' when you are talking about something that has not been mentioned yet, or if you are not talking about a specific thing. Once you have stated which specific thing you are talking about, you use the article 'the'.

For example: Connect *an* ammeter to a cell and a bulb in a series circuit. (This could be any ammeter.)

Now, record the reading on *the* ammeter. (This is specifically the ammeter you have included in the circuit.)

1.3 Adjectives

Comparatives and superlatives

We use the *comparative* to compare two things.

We use the *superlative* when comparing three or more things.

To decide how to form the comparative or superlative, look at the number of syllables.

(A syllable is the number of sounds in a word. So 'atom' has two syllables: 'a'-'tom'. 'Atomic' has three: 'a'-'tom'-'ic'.)

Words of one syllable use the pattern '–er, –est' for the comparative and superlative.

For example, with 'fast':   The red car is *faster* than the blue one. The green car is the *fastest*.

Words ending in –y also use the pattern '-ier, -iest'.

For example, with 'heavy':   The wooden ball is *heavier* than the plastic ball. The steel ball is the *heaviest* ball.

Other words of two or more syllables use the patterns 'more … (than)', '(the) most …'.

For example, with 'penetrating':   Beta radiation is *more penetrating than* alpha radiation.

Gamma radiation is *the most penetrating* form of radiation.

You can use 'less … than' and 'the least …' in the same way as 'more … than' and 'the most …' to mean the opposite.

For example: Beta radiation is *less penetrating than* beta radiation.

Alpha radiation is *the least penetrating* form of radiation.

1.4 Prepositions

Prepositions are important when constructing sentences. Prepositions are words such as 'in, on, behind, for, at' and so on. A preposition sits before a noun to show the noun's relationship to another word in the sentence. In science, we often use relationships of place and time in order to talk about the position and movement of things.

Relationships of place

> The car stopped *at* the supermarket.
>
> Put the Bunsen burner *on* a heat-proof mat.
>
> The pebble was immersed *in* the water.

Relationships of time

> The Hubble space telescope was launched *in* 1990.
>
> *At* noon, the experiment began.
>
> The sun sets *in* the evening.

Other uses

There are many other uses of prepositions. However, there are not really any rules for them and they often do not translate easily from language to language. Therefore we just have to learn them.

Common examples from physics include: We measure length *in* metres.

In gases, particles collide *with* each other.

Electrons are attracted *to* the nucleus.

There are many more and you should build up a list of them in your notebooks.

1.5 Changing words – adding an 's'

The letter 's' is very important in the English language as it has several functions.

Plurals

Most plurals are formed by adding an 's' to the word.

For example: A hydrogen atom has one proton while a helium atom has two proton*s*.

Possessives

Most possessive forms are constructed like this: noun + apostrophe + s

For example: *Einstein's* theory of relativity.

Note that the possessive 'its' (see above) does *not* have an apostrophe.

It's and its

It is important to understand the difference between *it's* and *its*. *It's* means *it is* while *its* is a possessive.

For example: A liquid-in-glass thermometer is made from glass tubing. *Its* function is to measure temperature. ('Its' here means 'the function of the thermometer'.)

Platinum is a very dense metal. *It's* denser than gold and silver. (Here *it's* means *it is*.)

In formal writing, which you should use in science, it is better to write *it is* rather than *it's*.

2 Types of sentence

2.1 Passive sentences

We use passive sentences when what is being done in the sentence is more important than who is doing it. The passive form focuses on the action, rather than who is performing the action. In science, the passive voice is often used in statements of fact, in describing processes, and in describing experiments.

For example: Mass is measured in kilograms.

Energy is released in nuclear reactions.

The charged rod was attracted to the cloth.

An active sentence follows the structure: subject + verb + (*usually*) object: Newton's laws describe the properties of motion.

In this sentence, the subject is *Newton's laws*

The verb is *describe*

The object is *the properties of motion*

To make the sentence passive we follow some simple steps:

1   We start the sentence with the *object* of the sentence. *This object becomes the new subject.*

2   We choose a form of the verb 'to be'. The form of the verb you chose should match the tense of the verb in the active sentence. '*Describe*' is in the present tense and so we need the present form of the verb to be (i.e. *is* or *are*). '*Is*' is for singular objects and '*are*' is for plural objects.

3   We use the original verb but in its third form – the past participle form.

4   We decide if we need the original subject in our sentence or not. If we choose to keep it, then we must use the word 'by' to connect it to the sentence.

Our passive sentence is: The properties of motion are described by Newton's laws.

How do we decide if we need the original subject?

Look at this example: People measure temperatures using thermometers. (active)

Temperatures are measured using thermometers (by people). (passive)

It makes no sense to add 'by people' as this is obvious. It is quite common in science not to include the original subject.

2.2 Conditional sentences

The most common forms of conditional sentences are sentences that begin with the word 'if'.

Zero conditional

The *zero conditional* is used for facts and truths. In science, you would also use the zero conditional to state the conclusion of an experiment.

Formed using: *If + present simple, + present simple*

For example: *If* you *heat* ice, it *melts*.

If ice *is heated*, it *melts*.

First conditional

The *first conditional* is used for things that are a consequence of an action. In science, the first conditional is often used for predictions.

Formed using: *If + present simple, + will + the infinitive*

For example   *If* you *burn* coal, you *will pollute* the atmosphere.

If more weights *are added*, the spring *will extend* further.

In addition to 'will', we can use other modal verbs such as 'can' and 'may' in a first conditional sentence. Using 'can' and 'may' makes the statement less certain, or less probable.

Second conditional

The *second conditional* is used for situations that are possible but unlikely. In science, you might use the second conditional in discussing how a situation or process would be different if you changed the conditions.

Formed using: *If + past simple, + would + the infinitive*

For example: *If* you *studied* more, you *would pass* the exam. (The student is unlikely to study more).

Third conditional

The *third conditional* is used for actions that did not happen. In science, it is useful when evaluating experiments.

Formed using: *If + past perfect, would + have + a past participle.*

(The *past perfect* is made using *had + a past participle*.)

For example: *If* we *had used* a micrometer instead of a ruler, we *would have measured* the thickness of the wire more accurately.

As well as 'would', we can use other modal verbs such as 'could' and 'might'.

2.3 Relative clauses

Sentences can have more than one part, or clause. We often use *defining relative clauses* where:

- the first part of the sentence introduces a word or thing (main clause)
- the second part of the sentence gives a definition of that word or thing (defining relative clause).

The two parts of the sentence are linked by a word such as 'which', 'that', 'whose', 'when', and so on.

We use defining relative clauses in science to write clear definitions. When writing these definitions, it is helpful to think about these headings:

The article (a/an or the); not always needed	The word or thing being defined	The verb *is* or *are*	The category the word belongs to	Which/that/ whose/ etc	The rest of the sentence
An	ammeter	is	an instrument	that	measures electric current in amps.
	Thermistors	are	components	whose	resistance changes when they are heated.
	Refraction	is	a process	where	light rays are bent.
The	Moon	is	a satellite	which	orbits the Earth.